Parish Life Coordinators

OTHER BOOKS IN THE
EMERGING MODELS OF PASTORAL
LEADERSHIP SERIES

Shaping Catholic Parishes:
Pastoral Leaders in the 21st Century
edited by Carole Ganim

Pastoring Multiple Parishes
by Mark Mogilka and Kate Wiskus

Parish Life Coordinators

PROFILE OF AN EMERGING MINISTRY

Kathy Hendricks

◇◇◇

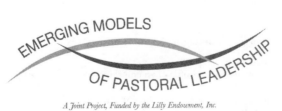

A Joint Project, Funded by the Lilly Endowment, Inc.

LOYOLA PRESS.
A JESUIT MINISTRY
Chicago

Partnering for Pastoral Excellence

National Association for Lay Ministry Conference for Pastoral Planning and Council Development National Association of Church Personnel Administrators National Association of Diaconate Directors National Catholic Young Adult Ministry Association NCYAMA National Federation of Priests Councils

LOYOLA PRESS.
A JESUIT MINISTRY

3441 N. Ashland Avenue
Chicago, Illinois 60657
(800) 621-1008
www.loyolapress.com

Cover design by Kathryn Seckman Kirsch
Interior design by Maggie Hong

Library of Congress Cataloging-in-Publication Data

Hendricks, Kathy.
 Parish life coordinators : profile of an emerging ministry / Kathy Hendricks.
  p. cm.
 Includes bibliographical references (p. 101–102).
 ISBN-13: 978-0-8294-2648-9
 ISBN-10: 0-8294-2648-5
 1. Parish life coordinators--United States. 2. Lay ministry (Canon law) I. Title.
 KBU2890.H46 2009
 254'.0273--dc22

Printed in the United States of America
09 10 11 12 13 Bang 10 9 8 7 6 5 4 3 2 1

Contents

Introduction

Mark M. Gray
Center for Applied Research
in the Apostolate

In 2004, The Center for Applied Research in the Apostolate (CARA) at Georgetown University was asked by the Emerging Models of Pastoral Leadership Project to undertake a national study of parishes where pastoral care had been entrusted to someone other than a priest under Canon 517.2 of the Catholic Church's 1983 revised Code of Cannon Law.

At the time there were a few existing published historical studies of the canon, case studies for parishes that had been entrusted under the canon, and a survey of those who were serving at these parishes. Yet there was no existing comprehensive study of trends in Canon 517.2 parishes nor of their geographic scope. Anecdotally, these parishes certainly seemed to fit within the notion of an emerging model. The research conducted by CARA verified this notion.

The necessities for the model are clear. Between 1975 and 2008 the number of diocesan priests in the United States declined by twenty-three percent from 36,005 to 27,614.[1] During this same period the total number of parishes declined by only thirty-six (or 0.2 percent).[2] In an era where priests are becoming less numerous and the number of parishes remains stable, there is a need for others to fulfill ministry roles. Many have already answered this call.

In 1985, the pastoral care of ninety-three parishes in the United States had been entrusted to someone other than a priest.[3] In the next fifteen years, the number of these Canon 517.2 parishes increased by 381 percent. Since 2002, the pastoral care of nearly 500 or more parishes in the United States has been entrusted to a deacon, religious sister or brother, or other lay person.[4]

In the research we referred to those people who had been entrusted with one of the many ministry titles identified, parish life coordinator or PLC.[5] Most often these PLCs have been religious sisters although this trend is in decline with the population of religious sisters in the United States dropping by 56 percent between 1975 and 2008.[6] PLCs today are more often either a permanent deacon, or a lay woman or lay man. The largest concentration of parishes entrusted to PLCs is in the Midwest. On average these are significantly smaller than the average U.S. Catholic parish and are more likely to have racial and ethnic diversity among its parishioners.

A wave of parish restructuring in recent years has slightly reduced the number of parishes entrusted to PLCs. However, this may be only a brief pause in the overall trend as in the coming years the Catholic population is expected to continue to grow and the ministry needs of this population will increase in step.

In the research, CARA was able to isolate four attributes within dioceses that are related to the likelihood of a PLC appointment being made: dioceses with fewer priests than parishes, dioceses with larger distances between parishes (often in rural areas), dioceses with more Catholics per parish (where closing a parish would lead to difficulties for the practice of the faith), and dioceses where bishops were open to the model (as Canon 517.2 clearly states, "If the diocesan bishop should decide . . ."). We found these factors to be additive, meaning that a diocese that shares all of these attributes will be most likely to have parishes entrusted to PLCs.

Statistically, the most important of these attributes was the bishop. To explore this, CARA conducted six focus groups with bishops between October 2006 and April 2007 in New Mexico, Wisconsin, New York, Louisville, and St. Paul, Minnesota. Each focus group included between five and twelve bishops from the surrounding region.

Not all participating bishops had direct experience with Canon 517.2 parishes. Among those who did, most reported a positive assessment of their experience with PLCs. However, most bishops also identify the PLC model as a less-than-ideal solution to the priest shortage, describing PLCs as a "temporary" measure until priests can be assigned as pastors.

The bishops described generally positive reactions among parishioners to bringing in a PLC. Some say that PLCs brought new life to parishes and new perspectives on ministry. A few bishops admitted their own surprise at how well-received parish life coordinators are in parishes. There were also tensions noted, including fear among parishioners that having a PLC meant that the parish would soon close.

In planning for the future, the bishops tended to emphasize the need to continually pray for and encourage vocations. Yet most said they recognized that they will likely need to expand their PLC and lay ministry programs in order to compensate for a decreasing number of priests.

The collaboration between bishops and PLCs was found to be important to the success of the model. In CARA's surveys of PLCs, many respondents reported substantial improvements in the positive nature of their current professional interactions with their parishioners, parish staff, and sacramental ministers compared to the time when they were first entrusted with the parish. PLCs that were introduced to parishioners by their bishop were *most* likely to indicate that their current professional interactions with their parishioners to be "very" positive. Also, the longer PLCs have been entrusted with their parishes the more likely they are to report that their current professional interactions with parishioners are "very" positive.

This book presents a profile of the ministry of these PLCs both in statistics and in narrative providing the most in-depth account available of this emerging model of parish life. It represents the culmination of more than four years of research, discussion, and collaboration by the partners of the Lilly Endowment funded Emerging Models of Pastoral Excellence Project. The six national ministerial organizations responsible for the project are:

- The National Association for Lay Ministry (NALM)
- The Conference for Pastoral Planning and Council Development (CPPCD)
- The National Association of Church Personnel Administrators (NACPA)
- The National Association of Diaconate Directors (NADD)

- The National Catholic Young Adult Ministry Association (NCYAMA)
- The National Federation of Priests' Councils (NFPC)

In Chapter 1 the role of the PLC and those collaborating with them are explored from the revision in Canon law in 1983 to recent examples of how this collaboration occurs on a daily basis in parishes across the United States. In Chapters 2 and 3 the profile of PLCs is presented along with descriptions of their ministry. Chapters 4, 5, and 6 focus on implementation of the PLC model, best practices for making the model work, and a perspective about the future of the PLC model in the United States.

Throughout this book readers will hear the voices of the people that are living this ministry model in their own words. These include that of the author, Kathy Hendricks, who served as a PLC in the Diocese of Colorado Springs. This volume also presents some of the key statistical data regarding the model, which was collected by CARA. Readers will also gain access to the most up-to-date and thorough discourse about the implementation of the model derived from interviews, surveys, and/or meetings with ministry leaders, PLCs, priests, and bishops.

Mark M. Gray, Ph.D., is Research Associate Professor at the Center for Applied Research in the Apostolate at Georgetown University. He was the lead researcher of the center's study of Parish Life Coordinators.

What Is the Canon 517.2 Model?

The Canon 517.2 model of pastoral care is based on the 1983 revised Code of Canon Law.

> *If, because of a shortage of priests, the diocesan Bishop has judged that a deacon, or some other person who is not a priest, or a community of persons, should be entrusted with a share in the exercise of the pastoral care of a parish, he is to appoint some priest who, with the powers and faculties of a parish priest, will direct the pastoral care.*

The basis for this canon is the conviction that participation in the mission of the Church is a right and duty of all believers. It begins with Baptism, is strengthened in Confirmation, and continues to be nourished through the celebration of the Eucharist. The Code of Canon Law affirms this calling in various ministerial areas, including catechesis and liturgy. It also encompasses the "care of souls" that takes place within a parish. This is an activity centered on the Church's responsibility to teach, sanctify, and govern the People of God. "Full care of souls" is entrusted to priests (Canon 150), but partial care is a responsibility that can be shared by many, including laity, deacons, and vowed religious. It is this collaborative model, and the baptismal call to service, that forms the basis for understanding Canon 517.2.

The Job Description

Pam Minninger, parish life coordinator of St. Joseph Catholic Church in Gluckstadt, Mississippi, describes her ministry.

Using the words "authorized," "empowered," and "granted," the Bishop charged me with duties and responsibilities in three main areas. The first of these areas is the preaching of the Word, and includes preaching the Word of God at daily communion services and Liturgy of the Word services; at Sunday services when no priest is available; at funeral vigils, wake services, or funeral liturgies outside of Mass; at the Liturgy of the Hours; and at the baptism of a child under the age of seven, in accord with liturgical norms.

The next area of responsibility is the sacramental and liturgical ministry. I was authorized to baptize children under the age of seven according to approved rituals; to serve as an extraordinary minister of the Eucharist and Viaticum, and as a minister of Eucharistic exposition and reposition; to administer sacramentals, such as blessed ashes on Ash Wednesday, blessing of throats on the Feast of St. Blaise, and blessing of communicants; and to present to the bishop the names of designated liturgical ministers.

The third area of authorization is that of the administrative ministry. This includes presiding over the parish pastoral and finance councils; maintaining parish sacramental records and issuing sacramental documents; the preservation and maintenance of parish archives; administration of parish property; and all annual reporting required by the Diocese.[7]

The ecclesiastical appointment of "a deacon or some other person who is not a priest" has taken place in parishes across the country for more than twenty years. The decision to appoint a parish life coordinator (PLC) is reserved for the bishop as one way to address the shrinking number of priests and the expanding Catholic population. As of this writing, there are 27,614 diocesan priests serving over 64 million Catholics in this country.[8] That's roughly one priest for every 2,300 Catholics. In 1965, this figure was approximately one priest to every 1,270 Catholics.[9] The numbers indicate a trend that is likely to intensify in coming years, as more dioceses face a shortage of priests. Implementing Canon 517.2 through the appointment of a PLC provides bishops with an alternative to closing or merging parishes due to a shortage of priests.

The appointment of a PLC to a parish is one of several responses that a bishop may make in order to meet the pastoral needs of the Church. The 1983 Code of Canon Law describes four ways of providing pastoral care that are different from the traditional one parish-one pastor model.

- One priest-pastor can be entrusted with the pastoral care of several neighboring parishes.
- The pastoral care of a parish, or of several parishes, can be entrusted to several priests as a team, with one as moderator.
- Participation in the exercise of pastoral care of a parish may be entrusted to a deacon, a religious, a lay person, or to a community of such persons, with a priest provided with the powers and faculties of a pastor to moderate the pastoral care (c. 517.2). This provision may only be utilized because of a shortage of priests.
- A parochial vicar (who must be a priest) can be assigned to fulfill a specific ministry in different parishes at the

same time—e.g., provide liturgical leadership or pastoral counseling for several neighboring parish communities.

These canonical provisions are not emergency measures or temporary palliatives. They are valid instruments of pastoral care, which can and should be utilized to the utmost for the sake of the local communities of the faithful. Indeed, when writing about parishes that are strained to the point that they cannot do their work effectively, John Paul II urged local church authorities to foster "adaptation of parish structures according to the full flexibility granted by canon law, especially in promoting participation of the lay faithful in pastoral responsibilities."[10]

This book focuses on the third of these emerging models—parishes served by a Parish Life Coordinator according to Canon 517.2. One of the best ways to illustrate the model's potential and its challenges is through actual accounts of how it works.

A PLC's Real-Life Story

Jeff Kelling broke new ground when he was appointed by Bishop Richard Hanifen to be a parish life coordinator[11] for the Diocese of Colorado Springs. His job was not just to be entrusted with the pastoral care of a parish, but to start one as well. In 1988, the community of Highlands Ranch was just beginning to develop on the northern edge of the diocese adjacent to the Denver suburbs. Growth predictions for the community were significant. This called for the founding of a new parish in order to accommodate the burgeoning number of households that were being established in the area.

Many of those living south of the county line were surprised to learn that they were part of the Diocese of Colorado Springs, not the Archdiocese of Denver. This made establishing an identity with the diocese another of Kelling's tasks. The diocese gave him names of several people in Highlands Ranch who had inquired about a parish. Through these key contacts, word spread that a new parish was being formed. An organizational meeting drew 100 people, and the seeds of the parish, soon to be named Pax Christi, were planted.

Father Dennis Dwyer, pastor of a growing parish east of Highlands Ranch, served as priest moderator, but there was no assigned sacramental minister. Kelling contacted two Jesuit priests who were affiliated with Regis University and Regis High School in Denver, and they agreed to preside at weekend liturgies. Two Masses were celebrated each Sunday in an elementary school gymnasium, and a Methodist community offered their facilities for meeting space and funerals.

As the numbers grew and the parish began to form, Jesuits at nearby Sacred Heart Retreat House also began to help with sacramental ministry in the parish. This allowed for a rotation of about seven priests, who presided at weekend Masses and provided other sacramental services. Growth predictions proved to be accurate. Pax Christi began with roughly forty households. By the time Kelling left his position thirteen years later, that number had swelled to over 1,000.

Ministries in a PLC Parish

Implementation of the Canon 517.2 model most often relies on the close collaboration of three distinct ministries.

Parish Life Coordinator: The person taking on this role—a lay woman or lay man, a religious sister or brother, or a permanent deacon—is entrusted with the day-to-day pastoral care of the parish. The responsibilities of a PLC are multiple and varied, and include the coordination of the ministerial team, both staff and volunteers.

The parish life coordinator is appointed by the bishop and ministers under the bishop's authority. PLCs have the cooperation of priests and deacons, and the assistance of lay members of the Christian faithful. She or he is the primary contact between the parish and the diocese, a bond of hierarchical communion. The leader's role is an ecclesiastical office, not a temporary deputation. Even though the parish pastoral leader is not the pastor of the parish, and does not have the "full care of souls," the office is analogous to that of pastor.

In an article on parish pastoral leaders, canonist James A. Coriden points out the importance of such a role. "Partial [pastoral care] does not imply a small or minor participation, nor does it imply that the sharing is temporary or an emergency situation. Indeed, a partial sharing can be the major share, all except the sacramental roles reserved to priests."[12] At Pax Christi, Jeff Kelling did indeed take on the "major share" as he drew the core of the parish together, arranged for parish liturgies and other celebrations of the sacraments, and initiated the growth of parish ministries. Most PLCs operate in the same fashion.

Priest Moderator: In this role, a priest is appointed by the bishop to supervise and collaborate with the PLC in carrying out his or her responsibilities. He serves in a supervisory capacity, while the PLC provides the day-to-day pastoral care of the parish.

A priest moderator is an ecclesiastical office that may involve overseeing the work of other parishes on a simultaneous basis. Such was the case with Father Dennis Dwyer, the priest moderator of Pax Christi. Fr. Dwyer was also appointed as canonical pastor of the parish. This was in addition to his role as full-time pastor of Ave Maria Parish, a growing suburban parish located in the same region of the diocese. Jeff Kelling is quick to point out the support he was given by Father Dwyer as Pax Christi was forming. Fr. Dwyer was available as needed for consultation and guidance, but left the decision-making up to Kelling. This created a comfortable balance of collaboration from the beginning. It also helped to establish Kelling's authority as pastoral leader of Pax Christi and freed Father Dwyer to carry out his daily responsibilities at Ave Maria. Research shows that such close collaboration between the PLC and the priest moderator is vital to the smooth functioning of a Canon 517.2 model.

Sacramental Minister: In some parishes, one priest is appointed by the bishop to serve as sacramental minister. In this capacity, he presides at the Sunday and/or weekday celebrations of the Eucharist and provides other sacramental ministry. He may also have other obligations, such as serving as a supply priest at other parishes, providing sacramental ministry at a hospital, or holding a full-time position at the diocesan office.

Some PLC parishes do not have an appointed sacramental minister. At Pax Christi Parish, for example, it was Jeff Kelling's responsibility to seek out priests to preside at weekend liturgies and provide other sacramental services. According to the Emerging Models Project studies, seven in ten parish life coordinators are responsible for scheduling sacramental ministers for their parishes.[13] In any event, the sacramental minister collaborates with the PLC and other parish leaders, particularly those involved with liturgical planning. Like the parish life coordinator, the sacramental minister provides a pastoral presence through his interaction with the community. Depending on his level of involvement, he also participates in other areas of parish ministry, such as counseling or catechetics.

The way in which these three roles come together is an interplay of pastoral care for a parish community, and is one of the most fascinating aspects about the Canon 517.2 model. The next chapter will look at who has taken on this role and what responsibilities are entailed in being a parish life coordinator.

◇◇◇

THE AUTHOR'S STORY

Before I wrote this book, I was a parish life coordinator.[14] I didn't seek this position. Nevertheless, the invitation from the bishop seemed like the next best step along my own ministerial path, one that began in Catholic education. It led from there to parish and then diocesan positions of catechetical leadership, consultant and writing work with Catholic publishers, and round again to pastoral ministry.

At the time that Jeff Kelling was hired to form Pax Christi Parish, I was serving as the director of religious education for the Diocese of Colorado Springs. In that capacity, I worked with Kelling and the four other PLCs in the diocese in providing assistance as they developed their parish catechetical ministries. Several years later, I joined the staff of Pax Christi as coordinator of ministries. Two years after that, when Kelling left, I seemed like a natural fit as his successor. I knew the people and the people knew me.

My transition into the PLC position was remarkably smooth. This was due, in part, to my familiarity with the role and with the parish. It can also be credited to those who laid the groundwork for the model. Jeff Kelling was one of the first to pioneer Canon 517.2 in the diocese in the 1980s. As a result, I stepped into the position without much question on the part of diocesan personnel, clergy, or parish staff members. The role was firmly established both in the parish and the diocese and, if not always understood by newer parishioners, it was generally accepted and appreciated by other pastoral leaders.

It was also to my advantage that I was well acquainted with the priests who were involved with the parish. I knew Father Dwyer from my work in the diocesan office and had worked on collaborative projects with the Jesuits at Sacred Heart Retreat House for many years. It made our collaboration all the easier to establish and maintain.

My appointment was an interim one. The bishop wanted input from parishioners about the long-term appointment of a pastoral leader and asked me to lead the parish through a process of transition. In six months' time I was to submit a report to the priest personnel board containing recommendations about the assignment of either a priest-pastor or another PLC. This made excellent pastoral sense as it involved consultation with parishioners and allowed for a re-examination of the parish's history, mission, and vision for the future.

The interim role did present challenges. As a temporary leader, I was cautious about making changes, despite the desire of some around me to do so. With a major construction project underway, I was also uncertain about signing contracts or making other commitments that would affect the parish in the long term. In addition, Bishop Hanifen asked me to discern whether I wanted to place my name for consideration as the pastoral leader once my interim appointment was up. There was a lot to do, and to think about, in a short period of time.

◇◇◇

2

Who Are PLCs and What Do They Do?

Sister Maureen Chicoine is parish life coordinator at Our Lady of Hope Parish in San Bernardino, California. It is an inner city parish that was formed in 2006, when three parishes merged into one. The 4,200 registered households form a diverse community; most of these are Latino. Sister Maureen oversees the work of one full-time and two part-time pastoral associates, a business manager, three religious education coordinators, four secretaries, a housekeeper, and a deacon. She also collaborates with two priests, who serve as sacramental ministers, and works with one or two other priests who preside at weekend Masses.

With eleven Masses taking place each weekend, in two locations and in three languages (Spanish, English, and Vietnamese), there is a significant amount of liturgical planning and coordinating to do. She attends lots of meetings with staff, clergy, parish groups, and diocesan personnel. The merging of the three parishes, she said, is a long process that can be fraught with conflict, so the demands of her job are great and varied.

◇◇◇

A Profile of Parish Life Coordinators

Religious women like Sister Maureen Chicoine are the largest group to serve as parish life coordinators. This has been the case since Canon 517.2 first began to be implemented in the United States. The 2005 Emerging Models Project report, "Understanding the Ministry: Parish Life Coordinators in the United States," provides the following demographic profile:

- More than six in ten PLCs are female.
- Forty-two percent are women religious.
- Twenty-five percent are permanent deacons.
- Twenty percent are laywomen.
- Less than one in twenty are religious brothers.
- About one in ten are laymen.

As the study points out, this represents a sizable shift in demographics from 1990, when women religious made up three-quarters of the PLC population and only twelve percent were male.

Figure 1 provides detail of the ecclesial status of PLCs through 2008.

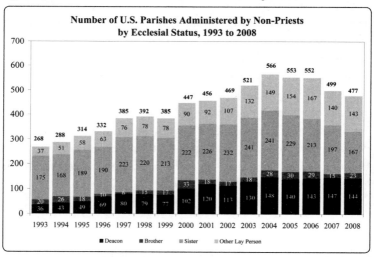

The 2005 Emerging Models Project report, which was prepared by the Center for Applied Research in the Apostolate, provides other demographic data:

Age: Religious sisters and brothers are among the oldest PLCs, with average ages of sixty-four and sixty-three, respectively. The average age of deacon PLCs is sixty. Lay PLCs are the youngest, with an average age of fifty-seven for laywomen and fifty-three for laymen. In comparison to the ages of PLCs in a 1990 survey conducted by Gary Burkhart, which was published by the Institute for Pastoral Life (1992), those PLCs currently entrusted with parishes are older than those serving fifteen years ago. In 1990, forty-three percent of PLCs were under fifty. By comparison, just ten percent are currently under fifty—fifty-eight percent are sixty or older.

Education: Ninety-four percent of PLCs indicate that they have attended a Catholic educational institution. Seventy-nine percent of PLCs have graduate degrees. Those PLCs who have graduate or professional degrees are more likely to be entrusted with parishes that have a comparatively large number of registered households. PLCs in 2004 have slightly higher levels of education than they did in 1990. Fifty-eight percent of PLCs have, or are in the process of, earning Master's degrees related to ministry, religion, or theology. Twelve percent have, or are in the process of obtaining, doctoral degrees in one of these fields. Deacons are less likely than all other PLCs to indicate that they have a Master's degree, but are more likely than other PLCs to say they have completed a ministry-formation program.

Training: Although highly educated, only a slight majority of PLCs indicate that their dioceses have a specific training requirement for PLCs (fifty-nine percent) or require ongoing formation or education for PLCs (fifty-one percent). Sixty-two percent of PLCs indicate that they have received some sort of specialized training for their ministry position (forty-one percent before they were entrusted with their parish). Although almost half of PLCs had no prior training specific to the task, two out of three agree "very much" that they feel adequately prepared for their ministry.

Experience: Before being appointed as PLCs, most were involved in general pastoral ministry (forty-seven percent), religious education (twenty-two percent), or they were a PLC in another parish (fourteen percent). Only thirty percent were in ministry at the parish they are now entrusted with before their appointment. Thus, most PLCs are not promoted from within a parish.

◇◇◇

WHAT A PLC DOES

When asked to describe her typical day, PLC Margaret Lima responds, "There isn't one. They're all different, and usually exciting." Mrs. Lima is parish life coordinator for Guardian Angels Parish in Kansas City, Missouri. She describes it as a "midtown" parish—"not exactly inner city, but definitely not the suburbs." There are 589 registered households, a number that fluctuates because of the highly mobile nature of the community. There are sixty different zip codes on the parish rolls, indicating that many people choose to attend from outside the parish boundaries. Besides Mrs. Lima, the parish has five full-time staff members, including a Jesuit priest who serves as associate pastor and an emergency assistance coordinator. Another position—the youth ministry director—is shared with another parish and subsidized by the diocese.

Mrs. Lima's days include multiple meetings with staff, councils, and committees. The parish recently initiated a $1 million campaign to renovate the interior of the church in order to make it handicap accessible. Construction projects are so time-consuming that they take away from more pastoral activity, something Mrs. Lima says she hopes to reclaim as the project reaches completion.

◇◇◇

What Is Pastoral Care?

The primary responsibility of a parish life coordinator is to "share in the exercise of the pastoral care of a parish" (Canon 517.2). What then is the meaning of "pastoral care"?

James Coriden discusses this question in his paper "Parish Pastoral Leaders: Canonical Structures and Practical Questions."[15] He says that the very description of the exercise of pastoral care in a parish includes within it the cooperation of others, especially the lay members of the Christian faithful. "This is of critical importance. In other words, the exercise of pastoral care is by definition a participative enterprise. As the canon on the pastoral care of marriage illustrates, pastoral care is the concern of the parish community, not only of the pastor (c. 1063)." [16]

He goes on to says that the *Code of Canon Law* does not identify the offices that entail the *full* care of souls, but it is commonly understood to include the offices of diocesan bishop and parish pastor. "Presiding at celebrations of the Eucharist, as well as at other sacramental celebrations, is integral to their pastoral leadership. The concept of the *full* care of souls was introduced in the 1983 *Code* to distinguish certain offices that are reserved to priests from those that can be exercised by deacons, religious, or lay persons (as in Canon 517.2). It is the canonical way of recognizing the participation of these persons in the exercise of pastoral care. It is a duly authorized and perfectly legitimate participation, but partial rather than full."

Father Coriden adds that distinguishing lay participation in the exercise of pastoral care as *partial* rather than *full* does not minimize or denigrate that exercise; it simply differentiates it

Summary: National Profiles of PLCs by Gender and Ecclesial Status in 2005

| | FEMALE | | | MALE | |
	Religious	Lay	Deacons	Lay	Religious
Average age in 2005	64	57	61	53	63
Married	—	45%	91%	80%	—
Race and Ethnicity					
Non-Hispanic White	93%	91%	83%	96%	100%
Hispanic/Latino	3%	5%	6%	4%	0%
Black/African American	2%	3%	11%	0%	0%
Formation and Education					
Has a ministry formation program certificate	26%	42%	34%	19%	18%
Has a bachelor's degree	100%	92%	73%	88%	91%
Has a graduate degree	95%	77%	41%	77%	91%
Master's degree in ministry, religion, or theology	53%	67%	17%	54%	36%
Had specialized training before starting as a PLC	45%	49%	29%	27%	36%
Appointment					
Appointed before 2000	46%	31%	26%	25%	45%
Introduced to parish by the archbishop	15%	13%	15%	8%	18%
Introduced self to parish	30%	14%	24%	35%	18%
Had formal installation ceremony	70%	73%	35%	52%	27%
Has a contract	59%	46%	44%	50%	64%
Has a job description	85%	87%	66%	92%	55%
Parishes					
PLC in more than one parish	17%	14%	14%	4%	9%
Average number of registered households	343	515	414	523	208
Average number of Sunday/ Saturday Vigil Masses per weekend	2	2.5	2.2	2.7	2.1
PLC's Roles at Mass					
Process in with the presider	46%	44%	96%	44%	36%
Offer welcoming to parishioners	64%	62%	54%	69%	64%

| | FEMALE | | | MALE | |
	Religious	Lay	Deacons	Lay	Religious
Remain in the sanctuary	32%	35%	91%	32%	27%
Preach	33%	39%	94%	39%	36%
Speak at the end of Mass	79%	63%	88%	68%	70%
Wear vestments	15%	16%	99%	19%	18%
Compensation and Benefits					
Median range of ministry salary and wages	$25,000-39,000	$25,000-39,000	$25,000-39,000	$25,000-39,000	$10,000-$24,999
Volunteering as a PLC	0%	3%	6%	4%	9%
Has health insurance as a PLC	86%	84%	76%	69%	64%
Has retirement benefits as a PLC	78%	89%	63%	73%	64%
Lives in the parish rectory	71%	31%	32%	27%	70%

as based on the Sacraments of Initiation rather than on the Sacrament of Orders. Not only can *partial* pastoral care be the "major share," it can also be quite stable and permanent.

The PLC's Responsibilities

PLCs provide pastoral care that is broadly defined. The specific tasks that a PLC carries out vary according to parish demographics and needs, but there are common areas of responsibility that constitute the exercise of pastoral care. Father Coriden breaks these into four primary areas.[17]

- Christian Formation—includes preaching, catechesis, education, and sacramental preparation
- Liturgical celebration and prayer—includes celebrating the sacraments, leading and teaching prayer, and giving spiritual direction

- Administration—includes detailed administrative duties
- Community Development—includes unifying, animating, and coordinating the parish community

According to the data provided in the Emerging Models Project report, "Understanding the Ministry: Parish Life Coordinators in the United States," the first two areas on Father Coriden's list—Christian formation and liturgical celebration and prayer—encompass many of the tasks that PLCs oversee. The following responsibilities were reported, in descending order of estimated time allotted to each area:

Christian Formation

- Sacramental preparation
- Adult faith formation
- Religious education for children
- Preparing or giving homilies
- Social justice ministry
- Youth/young adult ministry

Liturgical Celebration and Prayer

- Planning liturgy and music
- Preparation for presiding at funerals
- Preparation for presiding at baptisms
- Presiding at prayer services for the sick
- Presiding at daily communion services
- Presiding at a Sunday Celebration in the Absence of a Priest (SCAP)

Administration

- Parish budget and finances

Community Development

- Meeting with the parish pastoral council

While Christian formation and liturgical celebration and prayer involve a greater number of tasks, it is the third and fourth areas—Administration and Community Development—that PLCs say consume much of their time. Three-quarters of PLCs said that they spend "very much" of their time meeting with their parish pastoral council and dealing with the parish budget and finances. Sacramental preparation was another task that was rated as highly time-consuming.

Numerous other responsibilities named by PLCs are not covered by this list. These include involvement in diocesan and ecumenical programs and projects; service and outreach; social and evangelization ministries; visiting the sick and the homebound; developing leadership of pastoral council and finance committee; overseeing maintenance of parish property; overseeing communications with the parish; compiling reports for the diocese; representing the parish at deanery and ministerial alliance meetings; and participation in social gatherings.

One of the most vital roles that PLCs play is participation during Mass. This provides a way for them to be a visible presence in the community, as well as to collaborate with the sacramental minister. According to the Emerging Models Project surveys, the following are the most common actions that PLCs do at Mass:

- Speaking at the end of Mass (77 percent)

- Welcoming parishioners (62 percent)
- Processing in with the presider (56 percent)
- Preaching (48 percent)

As one might expect, deacon PLCs, since they are ordained, are more likely than PLCs of other ecclesial status to have active roles during Mass. Almost all deacons reported that they speak at the end of Mass, preach, wear vestments, and process in with the presider. They are less likely than other PLCs to welcome parishioners at the beginning of Mass.

Deacon PLCs are more likely than other PLCs to report spending "very much" of their time preparing and giving homilies, and preparing for or presiding at baptisms, funerals, Sunday Celebrations in the Absence of a Priest, and prayer services for the sick. Deacon PLCs are also much more likely than all other PLCs to indicate that they sometimes receive at least a portion of sacramental stipends.

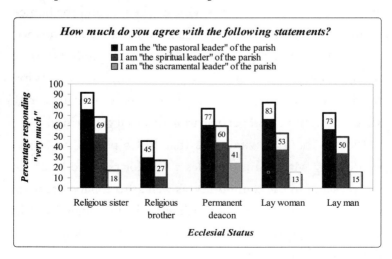

How much do you agree with the following statements?

■ I am the "the pastoral leader" of the parish
■ I am "the spiritual leader" of the parish
□ I am "the sacramental leader" of the parish

Nine out of ten or more PLCs agree at least "somewhat" that they are the pastoral leader and spiritual leader of their parish. Only half agree similarly that they are the sacramental leader, and most of those who do agree with this statement are deacons. PLCs that have been entrusted with their parish for longer periods of time are more likely to consider themselves the pastoral leaders and spiritual leaders of their parishes.

In the end, it is difficult to gauge exactly how much time is given each day to any of these responsibilities, as they ebb and flow according to parishioners' needs, seasons of the year, and availability of staff and volunteers. Then, of course, there are the unanticipated events that realign a PLC's work without notice, such as the death of a parishioner, the abrupt departure of a key staff member, or the untimely demise of the church's heating system.

Juggling multiple responsibilities requires extensive management skills, particularly those related to time management. The latter includes the ability to prioritize, and then to reshuffle those priorities as necessary. Flexibility is a key component of being a leader of a parish where the needs of the people, the expectation of supervisors, and the propensity for the unexpected is so prevalent. As one PLC put it, "the only way to carry out the job is to pray a lot and to retain a sense of humor."

◇◇◇

THE PLC'S RELATIONSHIPS

Deacon Roger Eberwein has been the PLC at Our Lady of the Woods Parish in Woodland Park, Colorado, for six years. The town is situated in a scenic part of the front range of the Rocky Mountains, eighteen miles west of Colorado Springs. In addition to the parish in Woodland Park, Deacon Eberwein is also entrusted with the pastoral care of two missions and a small faith community, all of which are located in more rural locations. Father Don Dilg serves on staff as sacramental minister. In addition, there is a staff of eight that includes two other deacons. There are four Masses each weekend, three in Woodland Park and the fourth held in one of the mission communities. One of the issues Deacon Eberwein had to deal with when he began his role as PLC was the departure of the previous pastor, who left not only the parish, but also the priesthood. It took time and sensitivity to help the community deal with their loss, as well as to transition to a new model of leadership.

The parish hosts a creative Web site, managed by one of the deacons on staff. It includes a blog for sharing information and initiating online conversation. Weekend homilies are available to download as podcasts. For communities that can easily have weekend liturgies affected by severe snowstorms in the winter, the creative use of technology is a further help in providing ministry and services.

Deacon Eberwein notes that his own leadership style emphasizes dialogue and discussion. This, he says, helps to avoid power struggles and focuses his authority as the pastoral leader. He and Father Dilg collaborate closely and each has a clear understanding of, and appreciation for, their respective roles. This creates a solid foundation for collaboration, a key component for the successful implementation of Canon 517.2.

◇◇◇

The PLC's work can be described in terms of relationships. Pastoral work is inherently collaborative, and the Canon 517.2 model involves the cooperation of many people in various roles.

The Priest Moderator

A primary relationship in the Canon 517.2 model is that of the parish life coordinator with the priest moderator. The role of the priest moderator is to oversee the work of the parish life coordinator. "This priest would necessarily work closely with the [PLC] in order to assure that the pastoral ministry truly responds to the needs of the people."[18] This relationship involves not only supervision on the part of the priest moderator, but also support. Therefore, it is critical that the PLC and priest moderator meet regularly.

The Bishop

The role of parish life coordinator is an ecclesiastical appointment, and it is important that PLCs have as much access to the bishop as any other pastor would. Depending on the size of the diocese, it may or may not be feasible for the PLC to have a great deal of contact with the bishop. In some dioceses, this is facilitated through the participation of parish life coordinators at meetings for pastors and parochial vicars.

As part of the Emerging Models Project, six focus groups from five episcopal regions across the country made up of fifty bishops were assembled to examine the issues, concerns, and possibilities stemming from Canon 517.2. The bishops at these forums had varying views about the place of PLCs at presbyteral meetings. Some felt that priests needed to gather as priests, and consequently they excluded PLCs from clergy convocations, retreats, and workshops, finding other ways to incorporate them into diocesan planning and the more business-oriented aspects of meetings for pastors and/or clergy."[19] In some dioceses, PLCs meet separately with the bishop once or twice a year. This allows time for concerns and issues specifically related to the role of a parish life coordinator to be addressed.

Sacramental Minister

The role of sacramental minister is filled in various ways in the Canon 517.2 model. In some parishes one priest serves this function, and he can become well known to parishioners. The role of sacramental minister may also be shared by a team of priests or by "supply priests" who make little or no connection with the parish community. In other cases, the sacramental minister is a retired priest who may welcome the opportunity to be involved with the parish while not having the responsibility of managing it. In all cases, collaboration between the sacramental minister and the PLC is crucial in making this model work. Not only do they need to collaborate on meeting the liturgical and sacramental needs of the parish, but together they also provide an invaluable ministerial presence in the community. For collaboration to truly work between the PLC and sacramental minister, there is a need for mutual respect and a willingness to listen, to engage in dialogue, and to respect each others' roles and responsibilities without defensiveness.

Parish Staff

Much of the PLC's time is taken up with the supervision of parish staff. These could be paid professionals or unpaid volunteers. In either case, the PLC oversees their ministries and their work, provides support, and evaluates their performances. It usually takes time for a new parish life coordinator to earn the trust and confidence of the staff, especially if they have worked with a previous pastor. It may be hard for some to accept a woman religious, deacon, or lay person as the pastoral

Working Together

Sister Justina Heneghan, RSM, and Father Philip Erickson have different ideas about pastoral care and ecclesiology, but they work well together at a parish in Kentucky. Sister Heneghan, the parish life coordinator, explains,

"Our model required a great deal of communication. We met weekly after Mass on Friday to review pastoral care issues. It was helpful for me to talk about the administrative concerns and problems in the parish. We shared stories and helped each other to resolve problems. At first, people would automatically go to the priest for everything, but Father Philip educated them. People would bring him announcements at the last minute, for example, and he would tell them that he would be happy to make the announcement if Sister Justina approves it. Then they would have to come to me. It didn't take long for the message to get across."[20]

leader. Thus, the PLC must both foster open collaboration and make difficult decisions when necessary and appropriate.

Parish Pastoral Council

The PLCs surveyed in the Emerging Models Project said that the parish pastoral council is the group with whom they most often collaborate in making decisions about the parish. Thus, establishing a good relationship with the pastoral council is an important priority for a new parish life coordinator.

Diocesan Staff

Parish life coordinators often note the importance of working with diocesan staff. In the course of their ministry they will work with all of the departments of a diocese—finance, human resources, tribunal, Christian formation, liturgy, Catholic Charities, and others. It is critical to know who to call for assistance as various needs in the parish arise. At the same time, diocesan staff must get to know PLCs and work to understand the scope and responsibilities of this emerging model of leadership. This is particularly true of those who may not be familiar with Canon 517.2 and the rationale behind it.

Outside Support

The great paradox of any type of pastoral ministry is that ministers can become very isolated, despite being surrounded by people. The people they serve and lead are not the same ones they themselves turn to for personal support—they go outside of the parish for this. For men and women religious, this support may come from members of their communities. For lay-women and laymen, as well as deacons, such support may be present among family members or close friends. In all cases, it is important to safeguard one's time in order to maintain a healthy balance between one's ministry and one's personal life.

Parish life coordinators also need professional and spiritual support. It is advisable for a PLC to have a spiritual director. Some parish life coordinators meet regularly with other PLCs in their diocese or region to share common frustrations, glean the wisdom of others, and share solutions to the problems and challenges of their ministry. These support systems provide a vital way to retain energy and stimulate enthusiasm for the role of pastoral leader.

Liturgical Responsibilities

All PLCs share a primary focus on liturgical practice. Data from the Emerging Models Project research shows parishes with PLCs have, on average, fewer Masses than the average U.S. parish. Nevertheless, nearly all (ninety-eight percent) of PLC parishes celebrate at least one Sunday or Saturday Vigil Mass each week. In addition, the use of Sunday Celebrations in the Absence of a Parish (SCAP) is not widespread among these parishes. Only one in ten PLCs report offering SCAP services on a regular basis. The priority is clearly to provide for Eucharistic celebrations whenever possible.

◇◇◇

THE AUTHOR'S STORY

The ink was barely dry on my letter of assignment as parish life coordinator before the first set of challenges hit me. During the farewell party for Jeff Kelling, the outgoing PLC, I received an emergency phone call. One of our parishioners, a man heavily involved in the Knights of Columbus, had committed suicide. It thrust me straight into a crucial role as pastoral leader—walking with parishioners through the landscape of tragedy, heartbreak, and trauma.

The next morning, as I was trying to catch my breath between Masses, a pastoral council member cornered me with a list of concerns about staffing and the parish budget. I scheduled a follow-up meeting so that I could focus on the grieving family and the liturgies for the rest of the morning. Weeks later, while meeting with the bishop, I expressed my frustration over the tension that seemed to exist between ministry and administration. He laughed and responded, "You sound just like the priests."

After years of working for Catholic schools, parishes, and dioceses, I was used to keeping a lot of balls in the air at the same time. Nevertheless, the pressures of the parish life coordinator role were intense. There were back-to-back meetings to attend and an endless number of groups to consult with and listen to. There were more people to supervise and less time to do it. There was the routine work to manage and the unexpected happenings that blew it all to smithereens.

Alarming questions that I had never considered before would occur to me in the middle of the night: Who ordered the palms and ashes? What legal procedures were involved in putting up a new parish sign? How much paperwork had to be filled out before a couple could be married? Happily, most of these details were taken care of by staff members and volunteers whose jobs I had previously neither fully understood nor appreciated. Although some things fell through the cracks, I learned over and over again the value of delegating responsibility.

I drew heavily on my professional experience for both organizational management and pastoral care. I also learned that being a wife and mother made me familiar with the challenges of a typical Pax Christi parishioner's life: juggling work and family, making mortgage payments, and the fatigue that comes after sitting up all night with a sick child. These experiences served me well. I felt accepted by the community from the beginning. This, in turn, allowed me not only to accept my assignment as a PLC but to embrace it as well.

◇◇◇

3

Where to Find a PLC Parish

Sister Mary Jean Morris is a PLC at St. Luke the Evangelist Parish in Bruce, Mississippi. The parish encompasses an entire county with a tiny Catholic population. The parish was started by a lay woman who had been invited by the Glenmary Home Missioners to establish a Catholic presence in the area. The community began with three parishioners and had grown to twenty-five by the time she left five years later.

Now Sister Mary Jean ministers to thirty families—about one hundred people. She also provides pastoral care for the Mexican immigrants who work the sweet potato fields and who occasionally attend the services at the parish. Sister Mary Jean is the only person on staff, and consequently much of her work involves training, supporting, and overseeing the work of volunteers. She manages the parish finances and spends a good portion of her time applying for grants and filling out fiscal reports. She also directs the RCIA, works with annulments, and delivers mission appeals to help raise money for the Diocese of Jackson and for Glenmary. Serving on the local Chamber of Commerce board is one way that Sr. Mary Jean provides a Catholic presence in the community.

◇◇◇

PLCs are found in a variety of settings—from small and mid-sized rural parishes like St. Luke the Evangelist to large suburban parishes like Pax Christi, Guardian Angels, and Our Lady of Hope. To gain a fuller understanding of how Canon 517.2 is being implemented throughout the country, it helps to look at the various settings in which PLCs have been appointed and how they have impacted everything from wages and benefits to job descriptions and ministerial interactions.

PLC Parishes in the United States

In the early 1980s, the Diocese of New Ulm, Minnesota, became the first in the U.S. to implement Canon 517.2 when Bishop Raymond Lucker appointed a PLC to the parish. By 2004, there were 616 parishes administered by PLCs in 115 dioceses throughout the country. The majority of these were situated in the Midwest. This statistic reflects a doubling of the number of parishes with PLCs since 1993.

The majority of PLC parishes (forty percent) continue to be located in the Midwest. The South has the next greatest number (twenty-eight percent), followed by the West (twenty percent) and the Northeast (eleven percent).[21]

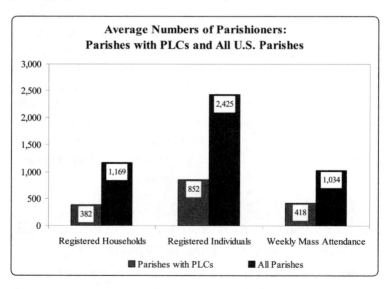

In his book *The Emerging Pastor* Peter Gilmour made an observation that may help explain the popularity of the Canon 517.2 model in the Midwest. Gilmour noted that "in the Midwest, parishes were established in almost every small town where there was a Catholic population."[22] These parishes built complexes made up of worship facilities, parochial schools, and rectories, and the people were used to having priests as pastors. Many parishes mean many pastors, and when priests became scarce, PLCs took their place.

Gilmour contrasts the Midwest to the South, where the Catholic population is too sparse to support a church in every town. Instead, one parish might encompass an entire county. The work of an organization like Glenmary Home Missioners—a Catholic society serving the spiritual and material needs of people throughout Appalacia, the South, and the Southwest—has given rise to a number of PLCs, such as Sister Mary Jean Morris in Mississippi. Glenmary has emphasized the training and placement of parish life coordinators in communities that previously had Glenmary priest-pastors. Glenmary's mission includes evangelization, ecumenism, and social justice, as well as nurturing a Catholic presence in the community. The apostolate seeks to serve in areas where the population of Catholics is less than three percent and to reach out to the unchurched and those who are poor.

The ecclesial status of parish life coordinators also varies in different regions of the country. Dioceses with the most parishes entrusted to religious sisters include New Ulm, Minnesota, Saginaw, Michigan, and Albany, New York. Those with the most parishes entrusted to deacons are Charleston, South Carolina, Lafayette, Louisiana, and Louisville, Kentucky. The largest numbers of parishes entrusted to laymen and laywomen are in Fairbanks, Alaska, Salina, Kansas, and Seattle, Washington. Dubuque, Iowa, has the largest number of parishes entrusted to religious brothers.

PLC Parishes Compared to Other Parishes

PLC parishes are typically smaller than the average U.S. parish as measured by CARA's National Parish Inventory (NPI), a database of parish life in the United States initiated in 1998 and periodically updated since. Nearly half of all PLC parishes have 200 or fewer registered households. Only seven percent have more than 1,200. As one might expect, PLC parishes celebrate fewer Masses and sacraments than the average U.S. parish and they also have smaller paid staffs. Including the PLC (but excluding sacramental ministers), PLC parishes average four paid staff. In the average U.S. parish, the number of paid staff members is between five and six. In the smallest parishes with 200 or fewer households, PLCs have, on average, between one and two other staff members.

PLC parishes celebrate several Masses each week. Communion services and Sunday Celebrations in the Absence of a Priest are not widely used at PLC parishes, although PLC parishes may be more likely to use them than the average parish. PLC parishes celebrate fewer Masses than the average U.S. parish—about two Sunday/Saturday Vigil Masses per weekend compared to about four in the average U.S. parish. Nearly all (ninety-eight percent) indicate that their parish celebrates at least one Sunday/Saturday Vigil Mass per week.

Spanish-language Sunday/Saturday Vigil Masses are celebrated with similar frequency in PLC parishes and U.S. parishes in general. Eighteen percent of PLC parishes indicate that they offer Spanish-language Masses. On average, PLC parishes offer significantly fewer weekday Masses—between one and two compared to nearly six in the average U.S. parish.

Seven in ten PLCs say it is their responsibility to schedule and arrange for the sacramental ministers that celebrate Mass at their parish.

Why Dioceses Choose the Canon 517.2 Model

The Emerging Models Project studies reveal three factors that affect the likelihood that a diocese will choose to implement a parish life coordinator model.

There are fewer priests in a diocese than there are parishes. This is the most obvious indicator: PLCs are more likely to be found in dioceses where there are more parishes than priests to staff them.

Large numbers of Catholics are spread over a wide area. Dioceses that are large in both population and square miles are more likely to have parish life coordinators than smaller ones. Regions such as the Midwest and West, where dioceses cover wide areas, are not able to cover all the pastoral needs of parishes spread miles apart with a single "circuit-rider" priest to meet their sacramental needs.

There are too many parishioners to justify closing or merging a parish. "Where the Catholic population is growing and the number of parishes is not, and the number of parishes exceeds the number of active diocesan priests, the likelihood that PLCs will be appointed is even more likely." One way that some bishops have dealt with the decline in the number of priests is by closing or merging parishes. This is a hard call in any instance. As the Emerging Models Project studies point out, however, it is also not feasible when the Catholic population is growing.

The lack of priests noted in Canon 517.2 is not just about numbers, however. *Serving Shoulder to Shoulder*, a document published by the Archdiocese of Los Angeles in 2006, points out that a "lack" means not only the number of priests available to serve as pastors, but also their "suitability and capacity" for the role. [23] "While ordination is a necessary requirement to be appointed pastor, it does not necessarily confer the abilities, skills, and qualities required for effective pastoral leadership."[24]

Wages, Benefits, and Housing

Compensation for parish life coordinators varies by region, as well as by ecclesial status and the size of the parish. According to the Emerging Models Project data, the majority of PLCs (forty-four percent) are paid between $25,000 and $39,999 a year. Eighteen percent earn more than $40,000 a year while thirty-six percent earn less than $25,000. Two percent draw no salary and work as volunteers. Religious sisters, laywomen and deacons are most likely to be part of the group earning the median salary of $25,000–$39,999. Lay male PLCs are more likely to earn between $40,000 and $59,999, while religious brothers are more likely to earn less than $25,000 (fifty-five percent). The largest percentages of parish life coordinators who earn more than $60,000 are situated in the West. Those in the South have the lowest salaries, with forty-two percent earning less than $25,000. The Midwest and the Northeast compensate the majority of PLCs with a median salary of $25,000–$39,999 (forty-nine percent and sixty-nine percent respectively).

Not surprisingly, parishes with larger numbers of households offer higher salaries—fifty-nine percent of PLCs working in parishes with households of over 1,201 earned between $40,000 and $59,999, and twenty-three percent earned $60,000 or more. Parishes with fewer than 200 households, by contrast, paid the majority of PLCs (fifty-four percent) less than $25,000.

Age and tenure also factor into the salary range in some surprising ways. PLCs who have been in their positions for less than two years are more likely than those with more tenure to earn $40,000 or more per year (twenty-five percent to fourteen percent). Younger PLCs are also likely to be paid more than their older colleagues. "Twenty-five percent of Vatican II and post-Vatican II generation PLCs earn a salary in this range compared to ten percent of Pre-Vatican II generation PLCs.

Parish life coordinators receive other benefits to the following degree:

Health insurance	82%
Retirement	76%
Paid vacations	68%
Paid retreats	56%
Dental insurance	54%
Tuition assistance	27%
Other	7%

More than half of PLCs live in the parish rectory, while another twelve percent are given some other kind of housing or stipend for this purpose. As might be expected, religious brothers and sisters make up the majority of those living in rectories (seventy-one percent). This is the group also more likely to receive alternate residential allowances. These housing benefits somewhat balance out the discrepancy in pay between those in religious communities and deacons, laymen, and laywomen. More men are likely to become PLCs in the future, because some bishops who are beginning to implement the model prefer permanent deacons for the ministry. At the forums conducted by the Emerging Models Project, bishops explained that they preferred deacons because of the theological training and ability to assume limited sacramental ministry. Indeed, in terms of ecclesial status, the percentage of deacons appointed as PLCs grew from six percent in 1990 to twenty-five percent in 2005.

No matter what background, experience, or education a PLC has, it is most important that he or she have a gift for leadership. The heart of this gift is vision. "The leader must be able to hold up and hold out a vision, inviting others to live with, in, from, and for that vision . . . [Such vision] is shaped by the word and the work, the meaning and the message of Jesus Christ."[25] Everything a parish life coordinator does flows from there.

◇◇◇

THE AUTHOR'S STORY

Pax Christi was a parish of affluent young families with very full nests. Most weekends, at least one of the liturgies included an infant Baptism. Funerals were rare, and generally associated with a sudden or accidental death rather than one connected with aging. These demographics strongly affected the role of the pastoral leader and the responsibilities that came with it.

Throughout my years as a catechetical leader, I knew that my experience as both wife and mother was serving me well. As PLC, however, this understanding was brought home in a very poignant way. My oldest child, Jenny, had died after complications from surgery a couple of weeks after her first birthday. While I was serving as PLC, a woman in the parish gave birth to a son with serious heart and lung problems. It drew me back to the agonized vigil my husband and I had kept by Jenny's bedside. In the course of reaching out to the family, I talked at length to the mother about the trauma of caring for a sick child and of the fear, fatigue, and self-doubt that is part of each waking moment. My past experience enabled me to offer the kind of pastoral care that may only be possible from one grieving parent to another.

In my role as pastoral leader I could also ensure that the appropriate parish services were extended to the family. These included bringing meals to the home, offering weekly prayers at Mass, arranging for the baby's Baptism, and providing respite care so the parents could have some time alone together. The baby was hospitalized for several months and then confined to the home for close to a year. It made for a long vigil that we, as a parish, were able to keep alongside the family.

In hearing the stories of other PLCs, I am struck by how each merges his or her gifts with the particular needs and situation of the community. While it is certainly critical for parish life coordinators to have the appropriate background, education, and experience for the role, they also need to have the heart for the work. I found my own surfacing through the ministry to a sick baby and his distraught parents. It was a sacred opportunity to be of service, to provide comfort, and to extend compassionate care. This made all the other, more humdrum aspects of the job well worth it.

◇◇◇

4

Implementing the Canon 517.2 Model

Successful implementation of the Canon 517.2 model is a substantial administrative and pastoral task involving the diocese, the parish staff, and parishioners. The first part of this chapter highlights several implementation issues of particular importance: criteria for designating PLC parishes, and the qualities that are especially desirable in applicants for a PLC position. The second part contains a checklist summarizing the implementation process.

During the winter of 2007, two research symposia were conducted by the Emerging Models of Pastoral Leadership Project. One hundred parish life coordinators, priest supervisors, sacramental ministers, and canon lawyers gathered to discover best practices for those ministering under Canon 517.2. They provided excellent insights into the implementation of the Canon 517.2 model and developed a list of best practices that serve as the groundwork for developing criteria and standards for this model of leadership.

Criteria for Designating a PLC Parish

The Canon 517.2 model has been successfully implemented in parishes of all kinds: rural, urban, suburban, large, small. Several criteria are especially important for success. One obvious necessity is adequate financial resources to support a parish life coordinator. If a parish lacks the necessary resources, the position may need to be subsidized from diocesan sources.

The document *Serving Shoulder to Shoulder,* published by the Archdiocese of Los Angeles, proposes four factors that are strongly associated with successful implementation of the Canon 517.2 model.

1. A good history of lay pastoral leadership in the parish. A parish is more likely to thrive under the leadership of a parish life coordinator if it has experience with lay ministry. PLCs have been around since the mid-1980s, and lay ecclesial ministry has been part of most parishes for decades. There are currently 30,632 lay ecclesial ministers working in parishes across the United States.[26] When parishioners have a positive experience of lay ministry, particularly with those in leadership roles, they are more likely to accept, or at least be open to, the assignment of a parish life coordinator. When the new PLC has worked on the parish staff in another capacity, the transition to PLC leadership is more likely to be smooth.

2. The parish staff is open and flexible, and its members have engaged in continuing formation. Staffs need to be open and willing to accept a sister, brother, lay person, or deacon as the one in charge. This calls for maturity and a commitment to working as a team for the good of the community.

3. The parish has a history of good liturgical celebrations. Parishes that emphasize liturgy more readily accept the roles of the PLC and the sacramental minister in this pastoral model. The Eucharist is a point of unity. As stated in the *Catechism of the Catholic Church,* the parish is "the place where all the faithful can be gathered together for the Sunday celebration of the Eucharist."[27]

4. The parish has a functioning parish pastoral council and finance committee. Having such groups functioning in a strong and effective manner is key to the success of a PLC parish. An effective pastoral council is more than a rubber stamp committee for a pastor or parish life coordinator. It is an important consultative body that serves a vital pastoral function. Likewise, an effective finance committee guides the parish in the wise use of its fiscal resources, so that there will be a future for the community. A parish life coordinator, like the pastor, has the right to convene these groups. The Emerging Models Project studies of PLCs noted a high level of consultation and collaboration with parish pastoral councils and other groups.

The Qualities of a Parish Life Coordinator

Those hiring the parish life coordinator are well advised to give careful thought to both the professional qualifications and the personal qualities they seek in this pastoral leader.

Professional qualifications include ministerial background, pastoral experience, and educational requirements. Diocesan guidelines for qualifications, such as those published by the Archdiocese of Los Angeles, are useful when they provide a clear, concise, and accessible picture of this model of leadership and its lines of supervision, collaboration, and support. Involving the priest personnel board is an ideal way to incorporate the model into an overall plan for pastoral leadership. The personal qualities of the candidate are also important. Choosing the right person for the role of PLC also requires attentiveness to the gifts one has to share with the parish. The Los Angeles document *As One Who Serves*, describes the parish life coordinator as "one who is designated to be the leader of a parish community [and] is above all the one who holds fast to the vision of the Reign of God [as] central to the meaning and message of Jesus."[28] This charism of leadership goes far beyond the role of an administrator. The document goes on to define three gifts that such leadership demands.

The first is **competence.** This entails not only knowing when, where, and how to take care of the daily working of a parish, but also a competence in ". . . theology, scripture, ethics, spirituality, Church history, and canon law."[29] The bishops who took part in the Emerging Models Project focus groups acknowledged the need for administrative skills, but they especially emphasized the importance of pastoral competence. Some thought that an academic degree in theology is desirable. Competent leaders get things done. They are aware of the details, but don't get bogged down in them. This is because they know how to empower others to bring parish plans and ministries to life.

The second gift is a **passion** for parish ministry, as well as for those who are served by it and who work in collaboration to provide it. A leader who is bored or burnt-out depletes the energy of those around him and drives people away. The leader with a passion for ministry ignites a similar passion in others.

The third gift is an **ability to communicate the vision** of the Reign of God. A visionary leader draws people to a larger perspective beyond the parish. Kevin Treston, a Christian leadership consultant, says that the starting point for such a vision is "metanoia—a conversion or paradigm shift in consciousness."

This allows the leader to "see with new understanding how God's dream for creation is being realized through our cooperation with the Holy Spirit . . . . This kind of leadership anchors the group's activities in the rock of firm beliefs and not in the sands of expedient leadership."[30]

Job Descriptions

Many of the bishops who took part in the Emerging Models Project forum on parish life coordinators noted the importance of having written job descriptions and clear expectations about the role. This, they said, helps to greatly reduce confusion about the responsibilities of the parish life coordinators and their relationships with sacramental ministers and priest moderators. In both the Emerging Models Project studies and symposia, respondents and participants concurred.

Job descriptions are just as important for sacramental ministers and priest moderators. By clarifying roles, responsibilities, and lines of accountability the potential for conflict and cross-communication is greatly reduced.

An Implementation Process

A gradual process of preparation and adjustment helps to alleviate fears and quell anxieties about transferring pastoral leadership to a lay person or deacon. One bishop noted the benefits of announcing transitions well in advance, in order to let parishioners know why an appointment is being made. Consideration needs to be given to how and when to announce the decision to the parish, the diocesan staff, the rest of the clergy, and the entire diocese. This information should include education on Canon 517.2 for all parishes, not just those with

The Gift of Rural Living

Sister Eileen Hurley, SCL, is pastoral administrator of three small parishes in rural Montana.

"The transition of leadership from priest to nonpriest was smooth. It was harvest time when I first arrived, which meant not many people were available to meet me, so I went to them. I arranged coffee gatherings at people's homes, where neighboring women and men could gather for a short time to meet me. This also gave me the chance to find my way around on the dusty roads of the parish. Thus, I began to discover the gift of rural living."[31]

PLCs. At least one visit to the parish by the bishop, preferably before a change in leadership takes place, is also desirable.

Parish meetings offer a venue for explaining the roles of the PLC, the priest moderator, and the sacramental minister as well as to provide a forum for parishioners to ask questions.

A Formal Installation Ritual

The involvement of the bishop in the process of announcing or installing a PLC has an impact on the way the model is received. "PLCs that were introduced to parishioners by their bishop are the most likely to indicate that their current professional interactions with parishioners are 'very' positive." The Emerging Models Project report reveals that sixty percent of parish life coordinators had a formal installation ceremony when they were appointed to the position. The larger the parish, the more likely there was to be an installation ceremony. An installation ceremony reinforces the ecclesial nature of the appointment and provides a way for the community to come together in prayer. It sets a hopeful tone for this next phase in the life of a faith community and is a powerful way to ritualize the parish's movement into a new style of leadership as well as to highlight the importance of collaborative leadership.

However it is done, it is important to take steps that will help parishioners see the appointment as a positive move for their community.

Best Practices for Implementing a PLC Pastoral Leadership Model

The research and symposia conducted by the Emerging Models of Leadership Project yielded vital input on best practices. Below are some representative suggestions from participants for successful implementation of the model.

Planning and Decision

Symposia participants emphasized the importance of adequate planning and preparation in ensuring the success of the parish life coordinator model.

Bishop

- Consult and plan for adopting and implementing Canon 517.2.
- Meet with the priest personnel board.
- Announce plan and prepare diocese for implementation.

Diocese

- Develop guidelines.

- Establish a link for parish life coordinator at the level of diocesan administration.
- Include parish life coordinators on the diocesan personnel board responsible for parish assignment and recommendations.
- Plan to include parish life coordinators in:
  » Diocesan planning
  » Meetings of pastors
  » Diocesan celebrations such as the Chrism Mass, Rite of Election, etc.
  » Deanery meetings
  » Diocesan consultative structures—e.g., an ex-officio parish life coordinator on the presbyteral council
- Establish a grievance process that enables the parish life coordinator to name the issue and begin the process of resolution on juridical matters.
- Delineate responsibilities given to the priest supervisor and the sacramental minister.

Salary and Benefits

Participants generally express the need to have guidelines set at the diocesan level for salary, benefits, and professional and personal development.

Financial

- Provide diocesan subsidies for mission parishes, in order to provide staff and just compensation.
- Set a diocesan salary scale for the priest supervisor and sacramental minister so that more wealthy parishes are

not able to "recruit" for a higher pay and leave out the poorer parishes.

- Research and establish diocesan guidelines for equitable salary, health benefits, and housing options.
- Provide benefit packages that include amounts for spiritual growth, physical wellness, ongoing education, retreats, retirement, and provisions for a sabbatical.

Ongoing Personal, Spiritual, and Professional Development

- Establish diocesan expectations for ongoing spiritual formation and spiritual direction for parish life coordinators and sacramental ministers.
- Schedule regular workshops for all ministers (parish life coordinators and priests) on needed topics.
- Hold regularly scheduled peer meetings with sacramental ministers and parish life coordinators to develop common practices.
- Offer diocesan gatherings of parish life coordinators on a regular basis for sharing, support, and formation.
- List available resources on the diocesan Website.

Selection, Appointment, and Installation

Selection

- Follow an open application process.
- Create a pool of candidates by consulting pastoral leaders.
- Conduct interviews of persons whose names have been surfaced.

- Develop a discernment process which includes interviews with a "selection team," references, etc.
- Include the bishop in candidate interviews.
- Choose deacon candidates on basis of competence.
- Select candidates for sacramental minister through a discernment process, including the parish life coordinator.

Selection Criteria

- Experience: Require proven parish experience, such as a term as pastoral associate, or equivalent experience, within a parish or school.
- Education: Require a master's degree in theology or equivalent.
- Select for gifts and talents as well as education and experience.

Appointment

- Have bishop appoint a parish life coordinator just as he does a priest-pastor.
- Conduct interviews with parish pastoral council and give their recommendations to the bishop.
- Send a letter of appointment to the parish life coordinator and to the parish community.
- Publicly announce the appointment—e.g. in the diocesan newspaper.

Installation

Research has indicated that one of the significant predictors of success is a formal installation, presided over by the diocesan bishop.

- Provide a formal installation rite with the bishop presiding, to install the parish life coordinator in the faith community along with the priest supervisor and the sacramental minister. Where this is not optimal, then the auxiliary bishop, vicar, or other representation of the bishop's office could officiate at such a ceremony.
- Include parishioners and parish staff in the installation ritual.

Preparation for the Canon 517.2 Appointment

Leaders at the symposia stressed the importance of extensive preparation for a Canon 517.2 appointment.

Preparation of Parish Life Coordinators:

- Offer orientation and formation for both new parish life coordinators and new pastors—twice in the first year of their assignment.
- Provide new employee orientation to the diocese, including procedures, training about each office, and orientation to policy and procedures.
- Provide an opportunity for a PLC candidate to shadow a current parish life coordinator.
- Assign trained and experienced mentors to both parish life coordinators and sacramental ministers for at least one year.

- Use the ministry standards for parish life coordinators developed by the National Association for Lay Ministry when designing the preparation process.

Preparation of Presbyterate and Diocesan Staff:

- Establish a formation program for the clergy so they understand the model.
- Educate chancery offices about this model, so they are aware and responsive to the need of parish life coordinators.
- Ensure that parish life coordinators formally receive correspondence given to pastors.

Preparation of Parish Community

- Require a consultative transitional process that provides for input from the parish council.
- Use the diocesan newspaper to highlight and educate about the role of the parish life coordinator.
- Make it a diocesan policy to inform the parish, as far in advance as possible, that a parish life coordinator will become the pastoral leader.
- Provide the parish with appropriate preparation, sermons, town hall meetings, follow-up, etc.
- Educate the parish that this is an appointment by the bishop and not a hiring by parish councils or pastors.
- Have the bishop or his delegate visit the parish and begin catechesis on the role of the parish life coordinator.

- Hold open meetings with diocesan personnel to clarify roles, policies, and financial issues and to discuss how the sacramental life of parish will continue.
- Offer opportunities for a series of dialogue meetings at which parishioners can hear the experiences of an existing parish life coordinator and sacramental minister team.
- Discuss what happens in the case of anointing, infant baptism, marriage, holy week services, rites of Christian burial, etc.
- Acknowledge, process, and ritualize the grief the parish feels about the loss of a priest-pastor.
- Have a Sabbath rest between transition of leadership, i.e., a two-weekend break before arrival of new leadership to give people and leaders time to grieve and breathe.

Supervision and Evaluation

Participants recommended that the implementation process include discussion of supervision relationships and the process for evaluation.

Supervision

- Provide for affirmation and support by the diocesan bishop, priest supervisor and sacramental minister.
- Clarify the role of a priest supervisor as delegated by the bishop.
- Clearly define the supervisory role of the priest supervisor.

- Provide for ongoing, regular meetings (at least quarterly) between priest supervisor, parish life coordinator, sacramental minister, and any mentors.
- Designate a contact person and process to work with the pastoral team if the relationship is not working.

Evaluations

- Evaluate the parish life coordinator, sacramental minister, and priest supervisor as a team.
- Conduct annual evaluations by the priest personnel office or another appropriate diocesan official.
- Develop a standardized evaluation process, similar to the one used for priest-pastors.
- Base evaluation on clearly defined job descriptions or ministry objectives.
- Use the National Certification Standards for Lay Ecclesial Ministers and the best practices for evaluations recommended by the National Association of Church Personnel Administrators.
- Emphasize professional growth and personal development.
- Obtain input from the parish pastoral council and diocesan offices.
- Share the results of the evaluation with the bishop.
- Have a pastoral conversation between the diocesan person/s responsible for parish life coordinators and the team (parish life coordinator, sacramental minister, and priest supervisor) regarding the pastoral care of the parish.

Pastoral Care of the Parish

- Evaluate pastoral care of the parish annually.
- Evaluate parish staff annually.
- Plan and review parish ministries, including input from parish leadership.
- Work with parish ministry leaders to evaluate parish programs and policies for effectiveness.

Liturgical Ministries

Participants in the symposia believe that training in liturgical ministries is essential for the parish life coordinator, the sacramental minister, and the parish liturgy committee.

Training

- Provide for a well-trained liturgist where feasible.
- Provide initial and ongoing training for:
  - » Shaping the liturgical life of the parish community.
  - » Presiding at a variety of prayer experiences in a way that offers warmth and sensitivity to the community.
  - » Preaching at liturgical services.
- Provide education/support for members of the liturgy committee.

Preparation for Liturgies and Sacramental Rituals

- Ensure that the parish life coordinator is responsible for good liturgies, investing the necessary time and resources into planning, music, and preparation.
- Ensure ongoing formation of liturgical ministers.
- Engage the sacramental minister in preparation as well as in the celebrations.

Liturgical Role of Parish Life Coordinator

- Ensure preparation for sacraments.
- Inaugurate the liturgical seasons and special feast days, calling the community to the spirit of the season.
- Offer greeting and welcome at beginning of liturgy.
- Make announcements and share news, such as what is happening in the diocese, to help the parishioners feel that they are part of a larger church.
- Function in a liturgical role at parish celebrations when the bishop is present.
- Preside at enrollment rites during Eucharistic celebrations.
- Creatively share role with sacramental minister in all appropriate liturgical rites—i.e., funerals and baptisms.
- Stand at the door of church after Mass with sacramental minister.

Preaching and Sacramental Ministries

The preaching role of the parish life coordinator is a sensitive and important topic. Participants at the symposia reflected on the specific times when the parish life coordinator would be called to preach. Their preaching would allow the community to hear God's Word through the lens of the parish life coordinator. Some expressed the belief that it is integral to the role of the parish pastoral leader and imperative that the parish life coordinator preach frequently when the community is gathered.

Participants believed that preaching by the parish life coordinator should be established and authorized whenever appropriate and possible, and that the rule that prevents the parish life coordinator from preaching at the Eucharist admits of exceptions, even regular exceptions.

- Have the parish life coordinator share the preaching ministry, in rotation with the sacramental minister and the deacon, at the Sunday Eucharist after the proclamation of the Gospel.
- Have the parish life coordinator be the ordinary preacher at non-Eucharistic liturgies, weddings, funeral masses, and other gatherings of the community.
- Catechize the assembly to understand the preaching role of the parish life coordinator.
- Establish diocesan, competency-based criteria for the preaching by the parish life coordinator.
- Have sacramental ministers and parish life coordinators reference and affirm one another in their preaching.

Authorization

- Recognize and affirm the possibilities within the law to allow lay preaching by appointed pastoral leaders.
- When requested by the bishop or the sacramental minister, authorize the parish life coordinator to reflect on the Sunday reading through the Scripture.
- Grant emergency faculties to the parish life coordinator to administer baptism, anointing of the sick, and marriage.

Role of Sacramental Minister

- Preside at sacramental liturgies.
- Oversee the areas of need in regard to sacraments: visiting of the sick, liturgical life, etc.

- Collaborate with the parish life coordinator, and other ministry leaders, to assess sacramental needs of the parish and how to fulfill them.

Other Parish Ministries

Participants expect the parish life coordinator to lead the development of a strong internal parish organizational structure involving the parish pastoral council, as well as various parish ministries.

- Work with the sacramental minister to articulate how they will collaborate and work together on pastoral ministry.
- Coordinate and oversee the ministry of all members of the parish staff, as well as all parish groups and organizations in consultation with respective advisory bodies.
- Encourage broad intra-parish communication.
- Empower the leadership of parishioners.
- Provide for the supervision and coordination of all parish education, spiritual, and service programs.
- Appoint a designated ministry coordinator who meets regularly with individual ministry leaders and then monthly with all leaders where feasible.
- Provide for spiritual renewal and ongoing formation for those involved in parish ministries.
- Gather with the leaders of parish ministries on a regular basis.
- Be involved in one-on-one relational ministry with ministry leaders.

- Spend regular prayer time with parish ministers.
- Commission parish ministers (e.g. PPC, finance, catechetical, and liturgical ministries).

Parish Administration

The parish life coordinator has the responsibility of calling, convening, and organizing the finance and parish pastoral councils. They have the same role as priest-pastor, excluding sacraments, and relate to these groups in the same way as the priest- pastor would. The parish life coordinator is backed up by the canonical pastor and the diocese.

Finances

- Provide oversight of finances with the aid of a business manager or bookkeeper.
- Develop a common finance reporting process for continuity of overall parish fiscal condition.

Parish Pastoral Councils

- Work with pastoral council to develop a comprehensive strategic plan, both for the administration and the spiritual life of the parish.
- Make final decision in all temporal matters after consultation.

Training

- Ensure initial and ongoing board and council training.
- Establish well-documented council roles and responsibilities.

- Train council members about the roles of the parish life coordinator, sacramental minister, and priest supervisor.

Other Ministries

- Empower parish leaders to lead and/or be present at various meetings so that the parish life coordinator does not have to be present at all meetings.
- Make an appearance at as many meetings as possible as a sign of support.
- Utilizes diocesan resources and services.

Other Recommendations

- Document the bishop's responsibilities with regard to Canon 517.2 and standardize it across the USCCB.
- Create a means for providing pastoral continuity at change of bishop—out of respect and justice for the position of the parish life coordinator as an ecclesiastical office.
- If deacons are the preferred choice, their training and Ensure the training and competence of deacons if deacons are the preferred choice.
- Hold regional gatherings of parish life coordinators should be held.

◇◇◇

THE AUTHOR'S STORY

Pastoral leaders rarely hear from parishioners when things are going well. One typo in the bulletin can draw more comment than a balanced budget or thoughtfully planned weekend liturgies. That's why I paid special attention to a voice mail message that landed on my phone after the celebration of All Saints Day. It was left by a mother who described how moved her fourteen-year-old daughter had been by the singing of the choir, the celebration of the Eucharist, and by the reflection I had offered. She said her daughter expressed a desire to go to church more regularly because it made her so happy to be there.

The administrative details that came with the PLC work sometimes left me feeling overwhelmed and exhausted, but my work with the parish liturgies always enlivened me. I generally preached once a month. The bishop had no objection to PLCs preaching on occasion and the priests who served as sacramental ministers at Pax Christi were equally open to this. The connection I made with parishioners at these and other liturgies was very important. My role as the pastoral leader was certainly solidified by my presence alongside the sacramental minister.

As the parish moved through the transition process as requested by the bishop, one common concern surfaced repeatedly in the consultations and meetings that took place. While some people were adamant about having a priest as pastor, and others wanted to retain the Canon 517.2 model, there was general agreement that the parish needed a strong spiritual leader. A mother's phone message had assured me that I was able to fulfill that role in the time I served as PLC.

◇◇◇

5

Making the Canon
517.2 Model Work

Sister Susan Slater is parish life coordinator[32] of St. Stephen Martyr Parish, located in the Los Angeles suburb of Monterey Park. The parish regularly serves a multicultural population of about 2000 people, 1,600 of whom are officially registered. The parish is about forty percent Hispanic, forty percent Asian (Chinese, Filipino, Vietnamese), and twenty percent Anglo. The pastoral staff includes Sister Susan, a full-time bilingual (English-Spanish) priest minister, and an Indonesian chaplain. Every weekend Mass is celebrated in three languages— English, Spanish, and Indonesian. Other staff members includee a DRE for elementary through junior high school; a Confirmation coordinator, who is shared with anotherr parish; a part-time music minister; an office manager; a business manager; and two maintenance persons. There is also a school with an enrollment of 260 in its K–8 classes, which will grow when a planned pre-K program opens.

Sister Susan's working relationship with the priest minister is a striking example of effective collaboration. She was on the parish staff as a pastoral associate when the pastor resigned. She was then appointed interim parish life coordinator, which later became permanent. The former pastor returned to St. Stephen's as the part-time priest minister on Sister Susan's staff. Their long-time partnership in ministry continued, even though their roles had changed. As Sister Susan puts it, "While we are clear on our roles, we consider each other as partners in ministry and consult each other frequently." They have reinstated a practice of meeting every two months for an extended time of prayer, sharing, and visioning, something that comprises an important part of their working relationship.

◇◇◇

Sister Susan Slater's story is yet another example of the many ways that Canon 517.2 can be implemented. Indeed, the parish life coordinator model has been implemented successfully in parishes of all kinds in the United States. A number of factors are associated with success. These include what can be called "best practices"—the must-do's of successful implementation of the model. There are also "better practices"—issues that need to be considered and addressed in order to generate a clearer understanding of Canon 517.2 and the roles, responsibilities, and relationships that it entails.

These ministerial practices are gleaned from experience and research. They are derived from the lived experiences of PLCs, bishops, priest moderators, and sacramental ministers involved in implementing this model. They are also drawn from Emerging Models Project questionnaires, interviews, and the results of the leadership symposia. Together, they provide a wealth of knowledge and insight into best and better practices.

Most of these practices focus on qualities of leadership. The responsibilities of a parish life coordinator's ministry require a significant mix of skills, abilities, talents, and gifts. This chapter will focus on these qualities, as well as on other factors associated with success in this emerging ministry.

Delegation

Whether serving at one parish or many, in rural, urban, or suburban environments, within a thousand-household parish or one with fifty families, the work is very demanding. Effective PLCs understand this. "Ministry is not something we have and offer to another in need, but something offered and received in mutual vulnerability and benefit. Ministry is a communal and mutual experience. We don't minister to; we minister with and among others."[33] Thus, an effective PLC understands the value of collaboration, the importance of delegation, and the wisdom of knowing when to step back and let others take the lead.

PLCs sometimes find delegation difficult. In his book *The Top Ten Mistakes that Leaders Make*, Hans Finzel lists three reasons why leaders are reluctant to relax and let go: fear of losing authority, fear that work will be done poorly, and unwillingness to take the necessary time to delegate.[34] Because of their enormous scope of responsibilities, PLCs can fall prey to all of these tendencies.

A new parish life coordinator, like other pastoral ministers, may try to control everything that happens in a parish as a misguided way to establish his or her authority. In fact, the opposite occurs. People become alienated and disengaged when nothing is asked or expected of them. Also, control-based leadership disregards the baptismal duty and dignity of the parishioner.

A PLC who is feeling insecure about the job might also refuse to delegate out of fear that things won't be done "right." This is an especially common trap for those addicted to perfection. Redoing the work of others does not foster involvement.

The third reason may be the most common of all. Delegation takes time, and it is often easier for busy PLCs to go it alone. Part of the vision that is enfolded into a model of parish leadership is one that encourages people to use their gifts. Delegation is one way to do this. Even though it takes time and forethought, the delegation of tasks to others fosters ownership and recognizes that it takes the gifts of many to carry out the works of the parish.

Communication

Miscommunication is one of the most common sources of conflict in an organization. For this reason, most books on effective leadership emphasize good communication skills and techniques.

Seasoned parish life coordinators agree that a crucial time for effective, in-house communication is when a leader first enters the position. When interviewed for this book about the advice they would offer to someone just moving into the ministry, each PLC stressed the importance of listening to as many people as possible during the first several months on the job. As one PLC notes, the cultivation of active listening from the outset helps to make it an ongoing practice throughout one's tenure in the position.

Deborah Tannen, an academic expert in communication, says that we need to be attuned to the "meta-messages" that are given when we communicate with others. These convey "meaning gleaned from how something is said, or from the fact that it was said at all."[35]

Meta-messages are especially powerful in the transition to a PLC ministry. Canon 517.2 is an unfamiliar and sometimes threatening model of leadership for many Catholics. Some may interpret the appointment of a PLC to mean that a parish is on the verge of being closed or that it is somehow not "worthy" of having its own priest/pastor. Parish life coordinators may need to develop thick skin in order to deal with the rejection that can occur when they are the first in their parish or diocese. Listening for the fear, hurt, anxiety, or confusion underneath the angry words or subversive behavior of parishioners, staff, or clergy can help broaden an understanding of how best to take on the role with grace and integrity.

Another area of potential miscommunication lies in the relationship of the parish life coordinator with the priest moderator or sacramental minister. Because Catholics are used to having a priest in charge as pastor, it is not unusual for staff, parishioners, diocesan personnel, or even other clergy members to initially seek out one of the priests for information or to circumvent a decision made by the PLC. The bishops involved in the Emerging Models Project forums acknowledged the importance of clear communication about roles and responsibilities. As one bishop put it, "If there are misunderstandings, they are part of what's an emerging ministry of the Church . . . We need to be able to solidify expectations, who's eligible and what needs to happen, and when a [PLC] comes in, what exactly are the responsibilities of each—of the priest moderator, sacramental minister, and so on."

Communication with parishioners needs to be maintained on an ongoing basis. Jeff Kelling, the PLC from the Colorado Springs diocese, made it a priority to explain his role continually throughout his thirteen-year tenure as a parish life coordinator, especially as new people joined the parish. It meant not only clarifying the position as an ecclesiastical appointment, but also assuring people that the parish was functioning just like any other Catholic parish.

Communication about sacramental services is often especially important during the implementation of the Canon 517.2 model. In parishes without a sacramental minister on staff, parishioners will have questions about pastoral emergencies. One PLC recalls the time a parishioner called the office about the death of her husband. The receptionist told her that the parish "didn't do funerals" and referred her to another parish. The PLC was horrified by this response and quickly moved to contact the widow about funeral arrangements. The incident prompted the creation of clearer procedures for staff to follow in emergency situations. It also led to the development of informational resources for the parish about sacramental services such as baptisms and weddings. In this way, parishioners were assured that the parish did indeed handle funerals and was ready to provide ministry for pastoral needs just like any other parish.

It has been observed that it's not so much *what* is decided in the Church that can generate tension and confusion, but *how* it's done. So it is with the appointment of a parish life coordinator. When the appointment is not announced in a positive way (or at all), and there is little or no communication with the parishioners about the reasons for such an appointment, anxiety and turmoil can ensue. People may leave the parish. Those that stay might continually call the PLC's authority into question. The parish life coordinator can feel like a stand-in until someone better comes along.

One PLC—a lay man who took on a difficult assignment in a parish that had lost a pastor due to unforeseen circumstances—described the continued slights that he felt. He worked hard to build trust among the community and his efforts seemed to be paying off. Parish membership was growing, and he had earned the respect and trust of the parishioners and his small staff. He worked particularly hard with the liturgy committee to plan a meaningful Triduum his first year as PLC. But after the Easter Vigil, he noticed the entire RCIA team gathered with the neophytes and their sponsors to have their picture taken with the visiting priest who had presided at the Mass. The scene reminded him of how difficult it was to establish his credibility as pastoral leader of the parish.

Providing Pastoral Presence

The PLC must delegate responsibility, while being perceived as a leader who is able to project a strong and stable pastoral presence. Many PLCs note how their presence at liturgies, parish events, and meetings provides continuity and reassurance. Jeff Kelling puts it well: "I was the recognizable face," he says. Parishioners wanted him to be present when there was a pastoral emergency, such as a death or illness. His consistent presence as leader was important in a parish with different sacramental ministers presiding at Mass each week.

Praying for the People

Patti Repikoff became pastoral leader of a parish after a beloved pastor had suddenly died.

"For the first year, I didn't do much else but listen and be present. I also engaged in a deliberate prayer campaign. I began a practice which I still use. Every night I would pray for the people on one page of the parish directory. I also asked people to pray for one page each night. This not only helped me to get to know the parishioners, but also to plant the idea of prayer as a path together in the parish. People were floored that I was praying for them and asking them to pray for each other. Over time, things improved."[36]

Most PLCs think that their presence at Mass is an important part of their leadership. The role of the PLC during Mass varies according to ecclesial status. Deacons are more likely to have an active role during Mass by processing in with the presider, vesting, preaching, remaining in the sanctuary, and speaking after communion. Even though other PLCs take a less active role in the Mass, there is strong case to be made for their visibility during these celebrations. As one PLC noted, "It is hard to be recognized as the leader of a parish if one doesn't have a significant voice at the occasion on which the community gathers—preaching is a must for PLCs. The community must hear from its leader in significant ways regularly and frequently."[37]

Practicing Collaboration

The Canon 517.2 model is essentially a collaborative one. Not only does it require the parish life coordinator, priest moderator, and sacramental minister to work together, but it also entails the collaborative efforts of parish staff and other leadership groups, diocesan personnel and clergy, and inter-parish cooperation and communication.

Collaborative ministry is one of the most rewarding aspects of the Canon 517.2 model, according to seventy-five percent of respondents to the Emerging Models Project survey. They mentioned, in particular, collaboration with parish councils and committees, sacramental ministry, and other regional leaders.[38]

The basis for understanding and embracing a collaborative model of ministry lies in the recognition that all Christians, through their baptismal calling, are to engage in the work of the Church. In their book, *Collaboration: Uniting Our Gifts in Ministry*, Loughlan Sofield, ST, and Carroll Juliano, SHCJ, define collaboration as "the identification, release, and union of all the gifts of ministry for the sake of the mission."[39] It is rooted in the understanding that every baptized person is gifted and called to share those gifts with the community in some way.

Collaboration is the best way to overcome the potential conflict and confusion that can arise around the roles, responsibilities, and relationships of the PLC, priest moderator, and sacramental minister. Collaboration, like delegation, requires a significant amount of time, patience, and energy. Parish leaders need to overcome the temptation to give up on it. Because the Canon 517.2 model is such a collaborative one, opting out of this component of leadership dooms it to failure.

Father Don Dilg, sacramental minister at Our Lady of the Woods Parish, frames it well when he describes the need, as a collaborator, to allow his thoughts and attitudes to be affected by co-workers. This not only promotes partnership, but it also guards against the "Lone Ranger" mindset that keeps all ministerial efforts running on parallel tracks. Eventually, the tracks cross paths and a collision takes place. No one comes out unscathed.

Three factors are especially important for making collaborative ministry work: *clarity*, *cohesion*, and *celebration*.

Clarity

Any parish situation requires clear direction around the different roles and responsibilities of those in charge. In a PLC parish, however, this may be all the more urgent because of the way Catholics are used to seeing things run. Clarity must begin with those in the key roles of pastoral leadership.

Cohesion

Very few parish life coordinators get to start from scratch. Instead, they inherit a staff, council, or host of volunteers who may or may not work together in a cohesive way. A key role of the leader is to draw upon the strengths of each member of the staff, team, committee, or group to help build community and foster a sense of dedication and commitment to the mission of the parish. This doesn't mean that the group has to work together on every single project or problem. Cohesive teams work together toward a common vision, while respecting, affirming, and celebrating the gifts that each person has to share. It also entails working together to resolve conflicts and to communicate with one another in an honest and honorable way.

Celebration

Pastoral teams draw closer together when they take the time to relax and celebrate their common identity and purpose. This can happen through occasional social gatherings or an annual retreat. One PLC notes how her staff celebrates a once-a-month Tuesday Afternoon Club, in which the staff gets together for an hour's worth of snacks and socializing. "It helps us all decompress," she says.

Whatever the method, healthy parish leaders draw their teams together to reaffirm their commitment to collaboration. "Good teams know how to genuinely laugh and to affirm one another. They take time to revel in the good work they've done and to recognize their mistakes as opportunities for growth. They understand celebration as a necessity for working together, not a luxury."[40]

Expressing gratitude to others is a critical component of both leadership and collaboration. Parish ministry is exhausting work. The time and energy devoted to it are often not fully understood by the average parishioner. Therefore, it is important for pastoral leaders to provide affirmation for their co-workers. Doing so builds trust, promotes ownership, and cultivates an atmosphere for caring and compassionate partnership.

Jeff Kelling attributes the success of one of his pastoral innovations to the social bonding that took place through relaxation. One of his most successful innovations was to initiate a ministry of adult acolytes at Mass. Because different priests presided at liturgies each weekend, the acolytes provided a crucial element of stability. They made sure the liturgical environment was set up properly. They also assisted the priests as needed and served as "masters of ceremony" by making announcements. Their role freed Kelling to fulfill other responsibilities, including preaching, greeting parishioners, and handling emergency situations.

Kelling believes that this ministry was successful, in part, because the acolytes took time to celebrate together. Besides occasional social gatherings, the group also attended an annual retreat together. Affirming their work and acknowledging the contribution they made to the parish kept their collaborative efforts active and engaging.

A collaborative relationship with parishioners is also gratifying. As one parish life coordinator expressed it, "The most rewarding aspect for me in ministry is the relationship I have with our parishioners. As a Franciscan, I walk through life building and experiencing relationships as a primary way to experience God. By building a relationship with our members one at a time, we have grown into a family-oriented church. Our people feel that our church is them, rather than the building."[41]

Building Staff and Parish Leadership Groups

The Emerging Models Project research shows that collaboration with parish councils and the parish staff is central to the PLC ministry. Collaboration with these groups tends to grow stronger over time. Building a team is an intensive undertaking that requires the commitment of each member of the group. This process of team-building generally follows a similar pattern.

Gathering: A time to get to know one another personally and professionally, to become acquainted with each person's role and responsibilities, and to gain an initial understanding of their working relationships.

Jelling: A time to establish norms for behavior and interaction and to set up structures for collaboration, consultation, and communication.

Colliding: A time to deal with clashes in personality, or styles of leadership that surface and create tension, sometimes escalating into conflict. Strong leadership is needed to manage conflict effectively.

Looking for Lay Leaders

Sister Maryellen Kane is pastoral life coordinator of a predominantly black, immigrant parish in Queens, New York.

"Since I am the only full-time minister in the parish, the development and mentoring of lay leaders for ministry is a top priority. The leadership of the parish is not in one person, but in the collective of leaders. Part of my role is to find and develop those leaders and to support the development of the collective leadership. One of the most successful ways to find leaders is through the one-on-one conversations."[42]

Teaming: A time to work together. Trust has been built and the group has learned how to cooperate in creative ways. "Many parishes assume this is the first step in collaborating. They start . . . with 'team building' exercises and activities long before the group has really named these as values."[43] In truth, "teaming" can only take place after the group has come through the first three stages in healthy fashion.

The stages of building a team are all the more crucial in parishes where Canon 517.2 is being implemented for the first time. It takes dedicated time and attention because collaboration between clergy and laity in this model is so significant. This is particularly important in situations where the parish life coordinator has been appointed from within the staff. According to the Emerging Models Project research, almost one-third of PLCs were serving in another kind of ministry in their current parish before being appointed to their canonical position.

There is an advantage to assuming the PLC position when already familiar with the parish and staff. But there can also be some problems when one is "elevated from the ranks." One PLC noted the difficulty that arose with other staff members when she was assigned as an interim parish life coordinator after the pastor retired. Some wanted the job for themselves. Others struggled to accept her authority after being her peer for several years.

Preparation for the change can relieve such problems. Diocesan offices could certainly help by developing orientation programs to help staff and other leadership groups learn about the parameters of the Canon 517.2 model, providing a forum for their questions and concerns, and offering guidance on building collaborative structures and relationships.

Changes in leadership sometimes trigger a certain amount of jockeying for power among staff members and other parish leaders, even with the sacramental minister. Ignoring or downplaying the situation is rarely helpful; it is best to deal with power struggles directly. Jeff Kelling advises PLCs to be confident in their role when their authority is challenged. "Never apologize for it," he says. "It is, after all, an official appointment." This isn't an invitation to throw one's ecclesial weight around. Rather, it is a reminder to take one's appointment of authority seriously and to assure the community that there is a pastoral leader in place who is capable of reaching decisions and directing the daily work of the parish.

Balance and Self-Assessment

All pastoral ministers are subject to the danger of burnout, but maybe none more so than the pastoral leader. There is a growing recognition that PLCs, like priest-pastors, need to go on an annual retreat that has been funded by the parish or diocese. The Emerging Models Project report, however, reveals that only fifty-six percent of PLCs currently have this as a benefit.

In the book *Spiritual Direction*, Henri Nouwen uses the image of a wagon wheel to depict the ideal integration necessary for pastoral ministry. He describes the hub as "communion with God in our heart." It connects with the many spokes of community and outward to the rim of the wheel of ministry. When we are too active in ministry, we end up on the rim, trying to take care of everybody's needs all the time. He notes that God invites us to both start and live in the hub. In this way, we stay connected with the spokes. Then "when [we] get to the rim, [we] won't have to run so fast."[44] Living in the hub, where they find a place for prayer, rest, and reflection, enables PLCs, sacramental ministers, and all who work to provide pastoral care to a community as a way to stop spinning their wheels and get to the heart of caring, effective, and faithful ministry.

In addition to evaluations conducted with staff and/or other pastoral leaders, parish life coordinators need time for self-assessment. Even if a retreat is not provided in a PLC's benefits package, it is crucial to claim such time—preferably with a mentor or spiritual director—as a way to undertake a personal evaluation and to discern one's continued commitment to the role. In his book *Leadership Jazz* Max DePree notes the importance of polishing one's gifts. It is an especially pertinent image for pastoral ministry because it entails reflection and a commitment to self-knowledge and growth. "Polishing gifts begins by reflecting on how to design the ways in which you as a leader . . . will work toward your potential."[45] It requires one to think expansively, to develop one's voice, and to unlearn routines that generate stagnation in a leadership role.

Clarifying Roles

Participants at the Emerging Models Project symposia for parish life coordinators and sacramental ministers said that the main difficulty in the new model is confusion, conflict, and lack of clarity over roles. Problems arise when the parishioners, sacramental ministers, bishop, or clergy outside of the parish do not recognize the PLCs as pastoral leaders.

The Emerging Models Project report shows that the acceptance of a parish life coordinator grows among parishioners with time. This isn't necessarily the case with priest moderators or bishops. One of the reasons for this might be the insufficient amount of contact between PLCs and priest

---

The New Model

John Klein, a permanent deacon since 1986, is pastoral life coordinator of two small parishes in rural South Carolina.

> "A priest in every parish is a good model, but appears to be no longer a viable one. If we don't get more priests, hopefully there will be enough people willing to work for the church to help it grow. I do not see a return to the old model, much as we would like. The new model has to work. People like me who enjoy the work and have the energy to do the work are necessary in the future church. Both the diaconal and lay leadership are definitely needed. I, for one, am willing to do it as long as I'm alive and able."[46]

moderators and bishops. When there is little chance to meet on a face-to-face basis, there is also little way of knowing what a parish life coordinator is doing to fulfill the responsibilities of her or his specific pastoral situation.

Even though a large number (ninety-four percent) of PLCs attend deanery or regional meetings, a smaller number (seventy-six percent) are invited to attend diocesan meetings for pastors. Exclusion from these meetings doesn't just leave the PLC out of the leadership loop; it also sets the parish apart from others in the diocese.

The bishops taking part in the Emerging Models Project forums were cognizant of the tensions that sometimes exist between parish life coordinators and sacramental ministers. This can happen when PLCs take on roles reserved for the clergy. It can also occur when sacramental ministers fail to honor the parish life coordinator as the one in charge of the day-to-day oversight of a parish, which includes liturgical planning. As one bishop noted, "When the sacramental minister comes in to celebrate, sometimes [that] priest may not be pastorally mature or sensitive and tries to rearrange the furniture every time he comes to say Mass and the parish life coordinator [finds] her authority . . . being shoved aside."

Another problem can arise when sacramental ministers are "drop-in" priests who have little or no connection with the community. One priest described it as being a "functionary" and another notes the energy-draining nature of such work. It can lead to burnout and low morale to be a circuit rider with no ties to any faith community.

Making Better Use of Evaluations

The Emerging Models Project data says that only forty-three percent of PLCs have had an evaluation on their ministry and only thirty-six percent of that number say this is done regularly.

In his survey response, one parish life coordinator noted that in three years, he'd never had any evaluation other than parishioners telling him he was doing a great job. "No one on a diocesan level has ever sat down with me to look [at] . . . the strengths, weaknesses, and opportunities that a true evaluation process holds." What this PLC is noting is a "best practice" that promotes personal and professional growth, hones skills, and serves the community.

It Takes Time

It takes time for new parish life coordinators and parishioners to adjust to the position. Anticipating some misunderstandings along the way can help lessen the tension and soothe the hurt feelings that can be part of a PLC's transition to the role. One PLC comments on a mistake he made when he approved an increase in fees for the religious education program. The DRE was understandably upset about not being consulted before the decision was made. "I realized I should have talked to her," the PLC confesses. "I would have reacted the same way." He tried to rectify the situation by apologizing to her at a staff meeting and assuring the DRE and the rest of the staff that he would strive to be more consultative. In return, he asked the staff to contribute ideas for cutting expenses and increasing revenue so that the parish could function in the black.

The initial period of adjustment for a parish life coordinator is a crucial time to listen—to staff, parish leaders, and parishioners. Consultation is key, especially in the beginning. As Hans Finzel notes in his book, a "top-down" attitude is a huge temptation for leaders, one that sets the wrong tone. If any institution should prize the model of servant leadership it is the Church. Listening and consulting are two profound ways for a PLC to introduce a style of leadership that is open, caring, and attentive to the pastoral welfare of the community.

◇◇◇

THE AUTHOR'S STORY

Pax Christi had a history of making decisions by consensus. While it is a great way to value each person's insights and ideas, it also can lead to long, drawn-out meetings. As PLC, I sat through some marathon discussions with the liturgy committee about whether the cross should be placed in a vertical or horizontal position for veneration during the Good Friday service. I have always considered myself sensitive to the importance of ritual and symbols, but the passion behind this particular issue escaped me. How was it possible that anyone could care so much about whether the cross was up or down?

Tempting as it was to intervene, I took a back seat and let the process unfold. The group finally reached a compromise and the end results were striking. The cross, large and heavy, was placed in a vertical position for the veneration but then was taken down and laid across the baptismal pool, symbolizing the tomb out of which Christ's life emerges. It made for a profound celebration.

The issue around the cross wasn't the only one discussed at these meetings, of course. Preparations for Holy Week were in the works before Jeff Kelling left his position as PLC. During that time, he had arranged for Father John Markey, a Dominican priest, to spend the entire week with the parish. Father John had presided at Masses on occasion and was well-liked by the community. He, in turn, was familiar with the way the parish ran and was open to collaborating with me and with the liturgy committee as we worked out the details of the Triduum.

As was customary at the parish, I wore an alb and participated in all of the services for the week. I preached on Holy Thursday, led some of the prayers on Good Friday, and assisted with the Baptisms on Holy Saturday. After the Easter Vigil, a tearful woman approached me to say it had been one of the most spiritual experiences of her life. It made all of the lengthy planning well worth it.

Looking back, I can see that a number of best practices were played out that week. While Father Markey brought his gifts as a priest, I brought my own as a lay woman and the day-to-day leader of the community. The work of the liturgy committee, members of the RCIA team, parish staff, and others made it a collaborative celebration. There was respect all around for each person's role and responsibility, a working together for the good of the community. This, in essence, is what any best practice of parish leadership should be about.

◇◇◇

6

The Future of the Canon 517.2 Model

The Emerging Models Project has produced an invaluable body of information about the implementation of Canon 517.2 over the past several years. The news about PLC parishes is overwhelmingly positive. Not only does the model provide pastoral care when there are not enough priests to serve as pastors, but it is also proving to be a vibrant way for the gifts of laity and clergy to be shared in creative collaboration and cooperation. New worlds of ministry are, indeed, emerging through the model. No one expects Canon 517.2 to become obsolete any time soon because the lack of priests that causes bishops to assign PLCs will be with us for the foreseeable future.

The widespread implementation of the model over the past twenty years has reaped some significant benefits, as evidenced by the Emerging Models Project research and the experiences of bishops, sacramental ministers, and parish life coordinators. It has also given rise to various issues as ramifications of the canon continue to surface. How these are addressed, both nationally and locally, will impact the future implementation of the canon. This chapter will address some of the issues that the church faces in the future as the development and implementation of the Canon 517.2 model continues.

Strengths and Weaknesses

During the two symposia for parish life coordinators and sacramental ministers sponsored by the Emerging Models Project, participants were asked to consider the benefits and weaknesses of the Canon 517.2 model. The participants thought that the Canon 517.2 model benefits the church in many ways. These included sharing the gifts of the laity, meeting the pastoral and spiritual needs of the people, and allowing priests to focus on the sacramental needs of the community. There were repeated references to the inclusive nature of the model through its appointment of women and married laymen to positions of pastoral leadership. The Canon 517.2 model was also described as a valuable way to prevent the closure of parishes and sustain the celebration of the Eucharist.

Symposia participants were also asked to list difficulties and weaknesses in the Canon 517.2 model. Some thought that it delayed discussion and decisions on important issues facing the church. The hopeful and creative aspects of the model are muted when it is seen as a temporary solution to the priest shortage. Participants wondered whether the use of PLCs created new layers of clericalism through the preference of deacons over lay people, and by lay ecclesial ministers taking on a role above those of other lay ministers. Participants also expressed concern that the role of priests was being diminished or obscured. It was felt that the opportunities for communities to celebrate the Eucharist and other sacraments would decrease as the shortage of sacramental ministers becomes more acute.

The bishops who took part in the Emerging Models Project forums voiced similar pros and cons about the Canon 517.2 model from their perspective as the key decision-makers in the process. Some noted with a bit of surprise how positively parish life coordinators were received and how they brought a new ministerial perspective with them. While acknowledging that the assignment of a PLC brought some anxiety—and even fear—to some parishioners, bishops noted the model has also provided an alternative to closing parishes. As one bishop said, "To put in a parish life coordinator has enabled [a] community to continue to exist and to have the sacraments. I haven't seen as many negative things coming from it as I have positive things."

Yet the bishops had their concerns. Most of those participating in the forums viewed Canon 517.2 as a temporary solution to the shortage of priests—"a stopgap measure until a priest can be assigned to the parish as pastor." This situation can be awkward when a PLC's expectations over job tenure clash with a bishop's goal of assigning a priest-pastor in every parish. One bishop observed that implementing Canon 517.2 and then removing a PLC because a priest becomes available has an inherently unfair aspect to it. The parish life coordinator, he said, would rightly feel as if he or she was "downgraded." Should bishops provide other assignments for outgoing parish life coordinators? If not, it should be made clear at the time of the appointment that the PLC is an interim role.

The Role of the Parish Life Coordinator

In the Emerging Models Project survey, parish life coordinators were asked to name the most challenging aspect of their ministry position. Their most frequent response had to do with their role. Some mentioned the relative newness of the position and the lack of clarity about its responsibilities and the relationships it entailed. Others noted its unstable nature (the "stopgap" view of a PLC), as well as ambiguity about the PLC's role within the liturgies of the parish. A few areas in particular are going to continue to impact the way Canon 517.2 is implemented and accepted within a parish.

Clergy and PLCs

Data from the Emerging Models Project shows that the longer the tenure of the PLC, the more positively he or she is received by parishioners. Thus, while there may be an initial resistance to, or anxiety about, the assignment of a PLC to a parish, it would seem to dissipate in time. PLCs do not report the same happening with their priest moderators or bishops. They sometimes refer to tension, lack of support, or futile attempts at collaboration with priest moderators, bishops, or other clergy.

The bishops also noted these tensions and the unresolved questions around the relationships between themselves and parish life coordinators. Some of this has to do with deciding how often and in what forum to meet on a regular basis. Should lay PLCs be included in pastor meetings or retreats with priests and deacons? If not, when and how do they meet with the bishops and priest moderator? Doing so is an essential way to support the PLC's role and the responsibilities that come with it, while also providing adequate feedback, guidance, and supervision. Engaging in dialogue about these tensions is a positive step forward.

This is consistent with the Emerging Models Project data that shows nearly all PLCs reporting that they feel supported by their sacramental ministers. This relationship of trust is a cornerstone in the construction of any community, something that takes time, patience, and dedicated effort. "One of the key ingredients in the process of developing one's capacity to trust is the possession of a high level of self-esteem. Trust evolves when persons feel good enough about themselves to risk self-disclosure."[47]

If sacramental ministers and PLCs work together over a period of time, each has the opportunity to let their role click into place and to thus feel more confident about who they are and what they are doing. However, when priests are assigned to cover a number of different parishes each weekend, such opportunities for professional interaction and contact are short-circuited. It leaves some priests feeling demoralized and makes the cooperative relationship with PLCs harder to achieve. Therefore, the future of Canon 517.2 not only needs to include greater consideration of the role of the parish life coordinator, but also of the sacramental minister who is central to its implementation.

Ecclesial Status

In 1990, religious sisters made up eighty-seven percent of PLCs. By 2005 that figure had shrunk to forty-two percent. By contrast, the number of deacons serving in the role was six percent in 1990 and had risen to twenty-five percent by 2005. The numbers of laymen and laywomen in the role have also risen (from twelve percent to twenty percent of laywomen and five percent to nine percent of laymen).

In some instances, the assignment of a religious sister to the position of parish life coordinator has a certain level of credibility among parishioners, who may trust her competence and authority because of her ecclesial status. As the demographics change, similar acceptance of a lay woman or lay man may be harder to achieve. Therefore, the future of the model will need to be part of an overall effort to further clarify the call of the lay ecclesial minister. Documents published by the United States Catholic Conference of Bishops that deal with the call and the role of the lay ecclesial minister, such as *Coworkers in the Vineyard of the Lord*, will certainly be helpful in this regard.

Preference for Deacons

Some bishops have noted their preference for deacons to serve in the role of PLC because of their training and sacramental faculties. This is an advantage, but it also raises questions. Is the deacon appointed because of his qualifications for the job, or is it because of his clerical status? If it is the latter, is this fair to parishioners, to better-qualified lay ecclesial ministers, and to the deacons themselves? Secondly, is the assignment of deacons as PLCs consistent with the order of the diaconate? Father James Coriden takes up this point in his article on the role of parish life coordinators.

> The diaconate is an ancient and distinctive order with unique prerogatives and functions. It is harmful to envision and utilize deacons as "the next best thing" to having a priest, or "supplying for priests" when there aren't enough of them around. The order of deacons has had

its own reality and dignity for centuries, and it should not be envisioned as a substitutional role in the Church's panoply of ministries.[48]

Liturgical Responsibilities

The appointment of PLCs has allowed for the celebration of the Eucharist and other sacraments in parishes that might otherwise have closed or been merged with neighboring communities. However, in many places there is tension over the role of the parish life coordinator in the celebration of these liturgies, especially when there is little or no direction from the bishop on the matter. PLCs do see their role in weekend liturgies as significant. As one put it, "The greatest challenge is leading the parish without having a public forum [weekend liturgies]. Our sacramental minister does not agree [with me] on most subjects and therefore does not support them publicly. He can undo a trend or direction in minutes, even though he is not the leader of the parish." In this case, the PLC does not want to take on the role of the priest, as some might fear. He is rather trying to assume his position of leadership, and recognizes that taking part in the weekend liturgies is an important way to do this.

Stability of the Position

"About half of PLCs agree 'very much' that they have sufficient job security in ministry." Many bishops consider Canon 517.2 as a temporary solution to the priest shortage. At the same time, they also recognize the problems that exist for PLCs when their position is so unstable. Beyond job security, the issue also touches upon the gifts that a parish life coordinator has to share, the investment the diocese and parish has made into his or her training, and the bond that he or she has formed with a parish community.

One PLC told of the experience of being replaced in his parish by a priest-pastor. Although he understood the bishop's decision, the PLC was left without a job and a faith community. People in the parish didn't understand why he didn't continue to attend Mass and stay active in the community. "How could I adequately explain how hard it was to come and sit in the back pew?" he asked. "I had preached and directed the overall operation of the parish." The experience left him feeling at a loss about where and how to use the gifts he had to offer. In a discussion with the bishop about the matter, he said the bishop did admit that this part of the Canon 517.2 model had not been adequately thought through.

A Happy Parish

Sister Carole Ruland, MHSH, has been a pastoral life coordinator of a parish in the Tuscon diocese since 1988.

> "What began as a stopgap measure has begun to exhibit genuine benefits. Our parish is a happy parish. The needs of our people are being well met. The adults are always ready to take advantage of adult education programs offered at the parish or at our local retreat center. Many new members speak of how open and welcoming the parish is, of how good it feels to be part of such a community. They often bring their family and friends to the church during the week because they enjoy showing off the parish. For many, it is more than the building where people gather on Sunday. It is a place that touches their everyday lives."[49]

Being a parish life coordinator is far more than a job—it is a ministry. The document, *Co-workers in the Vineyard of the Lord*, has a helpful description of ministry as applied to lay persons. It is not to be confused with the ministry of the ordained, but "is exercised in accordance with the lay vocation . . . By their baptismal incorporation in the Body of Christ, lay persons are also equipped with gifts and graces to build up the Church from within, in cooperation with the hierarchy and under its direction."[50] There are laymen and laywomen, along with deacons and vowed Religious, who are gifted leaders. A creative application of Canon 517.2 is to call these people forth in order to use their charism for the good of the Church. It is not, then, a choice between a priest or lay person, but an option for "cultivating, nurturing, and sustaining collaboration between and among priests, deacons, vowed Religious, and lay leaders."[51] In time, as the Emerging Models Project research shows, parishioners embrace such leaders. Therefore, it is imperative that bishops consider the appointment to be much more than a stopgap measure; it is a utilization of one's gifts for the good of the Church.

Developing Clearer Titles

There are approximately three dozen different titles being used throughout the country to name the "person entrusted with the pastoral care of a parish" in Canon 517.2. Some of these, as James Coriden says, are inappropriate because they are misleading. "We should try to avoid confusion of titles and ambiguity of roles whenever possible."[52] He refers to titles that seem to equate a PLC's job with that of a business manager ("parish administrator"), confuse it with the clergy ("parochial administrator"), or render it so ambiguous that no one knows what it means ("parish life collaborator"). As Coriden points out, "Names matter, and the role of nonpriests leading parish communities has been clouded by the lack of an appropriate title."[53]

The title of "sacramental minister" also has its limitations. Some PLCs say that the title is an ineffective way to describe the role that a priest minister might play. In some parishes, the priest minister is a full-time staff member. He not only presides at the Eucharist and other sacramental celebrations, but also heads up some of the committees and serves as liaison to certain parish groups. On the other hand, a supply priest is only at the parish on weekends. To call both a "sacramental minister" does not do justice to the scope of their roles and responsibilities.

Pragmatic Concerns for the Future

Along with the theological implications of Canon 517.2 are more pragmatic issues. These include finances and parish demographics, as well as how to best prepare for PLC parishes.

Financial Needs and Parish Demographics

The Emerging Models Project data shows that small parishes are less able to afford a parish life coordinator and to pay stipends for the sacramental minister. Nevertheless, smaller-than-average parishes are currently more likely than larger ones to have a PLC assigned to them. This may change in the future. It is easier to place sacramental ministers in urban and suburban areas than in rural areas. Also, larger parishes are better able to afford a PLC. In addition, some bishops are reluctant to ask a single priest to pastor two or three larger parishes. It spreads pastoral resources too thinly and puts too great a load on these pastors. Some bishops note that allowing smaller parishes to bear the brunt of the priest shortage places the Canon 517.2 model in a negative light.

The Emerging Model Project research also reveals that PLC parishes are more racially and ethnically diverse than U.S. parishes in general. At the same time, the vast majority of PLCs identify themselves as Anglo, Caucasian, or White. This suggests that, in order to keep up with the growing diversity of the Catholic population, it is important to seek a broadly diverse pool of potential candidates for the role of parish life coordinators.

Preparing for Future PLC Parishes

The future implementation of Canon 517.2 needs to include planning in a thorough and positive manner. Participants at the Emerging Models Project symposia on PLCs and sacramental ministers had a number of suggestions regarding the need for adequate educational resources, programs, and processes for different groups of people.

Formation programs for new parish life coordinators, as well as ongoing education for seasoned PLCs, that will help them meet the unfolding demands of the role.

Better information about Canon 517.2 should be provided to parishes about to be assigned a PLC. This should include transition and grieving processes for communities that are losing a priest-pastor or merging with another parish community.

General education should be provided to U.S. Catholics about Canon 517.2, as well as education about the roles of the parish life coordinator, sacramental ministers, and priest moderators. This education also needs to stress the bishop's decisive role in assigning a PLC to a parish and how the process works at the diocesan level.

Education at seminaries and diaconate programs that will provide information about Canon 517.2. Seminarians and deacon candidates should also receive training in collaborative models of leadership and in the development of skills for working as part of a team since many of them will likely work in this type of pastoral ministry.

Education and information for clergy and diocesan personnel on the Canon 517.2 model and exploring how this model fits with an overall vision of diocesan ministry.

National standards that provide overall coherence to the model and offer help to bishops in writing guidelines for their dioceses.

Drawing Upon the Gifts of Clergy and Laity

One of the benefits of the Canon 517.2 model most often cited is its potential for drawing out the gifts of both clergy and laity. Strictly speaking, Canon 517.2 is not intended to be an expansion of lay ministry. Rather, it allows bishops an alternative way to provide pastoral care when there are not enough priests to meet the norm of one pastor assigned to one parish. Nevertheless, the entrusting of day-to-day pastoral care to a deacon or lay person is proving beneficial in utilizing the gifts of all the baptized. Deacons, vowed religious sisters and

A Call to Ministry

Pam Minninger is pastoral life coordinator of a parish near Jackson, Mississippi.

"Most of our people do not understand their own personal call to ministry. I didn't. Most would never apply the term "minister" to themselves. Two years ago I definitely would not have applied it to myself, but now I feel confident in my role and I am continuing to develop into it. My validation is being with people at really important sacramental times in their lives, and at times when they need the Church in their lives.

We cannot allow our people to dismiss this essential aspect of their call to discipleship by pleading, as I did, "I'm not qualified." We must remind them, as I am beginning to understand, that God doesn't call the qualified. God qualifies the called."[54]

brothers, and laywomen and laymen have different gifts to share. Bringing them into the arena of pastoral leadership is beneficial for the entire Church. As an Archdiocese of Los Angeles document put it, "As men and women who are neither ordained nor vowed Religious have continued to put their gifts to the direct service of the Church, we have grown in the realization that some of them have been blessed with a share in the gift of leadership. We recognize that they have been given a charism to lead the Christian community, responding to the needs of the Church and the wider world at this time."[55]

In their book *Building Community* co-authors Loughlan Soffield, Rosine Hammett, and Carroll Juliano stress the collective nature of gifts. "A community is a group of individuals who come together for a mission. Each member brings gifts joining them with those of the community to carry out the mission."[56]

Drawing out the leadership gifts of both laity and clergy also has an effect on the people they serve, as it calls upon others to live their baptismal promises more fully. "By Baptism, every member of the Church participates in Christ's role as priest, prophet, and king . . . The laity do this in the context of their lives within families, parish communities, civic community, and the workplace."[57]

While the role of the parish life coordinator is to draw out the gifts of the community, his or her efforts can be stymied either by co-workers and collaborators or by the community itself. The Emerging Models Project data illustrates how this can happen.

One of the challenges the Catholic Church faces as it moves further into the twenty-first century is the provision of sound pastoral leadership while simultaneously experiencing a shortage of priests. Canon 517.2 is a positive response to such a challenge, one that affirms the central importance of the ordained priesthood while also utilizing the gifts of lay people, vowed religious, and deacons in the pastoral care of parishes. It makes for intriguing possibilities as this emerging model of leadership continues to develop.

◇◇◇

THE AUTHOR'S STORY

A few months after being appointed parish life coordinator at Pax Christi, I received a phone call from one of the mothers in the parish. Her daughter, a high school student, wanted to know if she could shadow me for a day as part of "Take Your Daughter to Work Day." I don't know how much the young woman learned about parish ministry by trailing after me for a day, but the fact that she wanted to know more about my role was significant.

On another occasion, a young man in his late teens approached me after Mass and told me how much he appreciated it when I preached. He referred to a reflection I gave on the feast of the Transfiguration, in which I said I could understand why the disciples wanted to stay on the mountaintop—it was much easier than descending back into the painful realities of life. He went on to tell me how the reflection helped him deal with the death of his sister. Both of these experiences stand out as highlights of my PLC experience.

After a great deal of discernment, I decided against being considered for the permanent PLC job. The construction of the new worship facilities and the capital campaign that was needed to fund it were going to be major parts of the new leader's work. This was not where my heart was.

My last weekend as parish life coordinator included a party and a touching tribute from the pastoral council. I also received several lovely expressions of gratitude. No one mentioned the work I had put into preparing budgets or convening meetings. Instead, they acknowledged the times I had been present when it was most needed and the ways I had touched their lives. It reinforced for me what really matters to those we serve as well as what makes an effective pastoral leader.

When I look back on my brief tenure as a PLC, it is the opportunities to be present to people in the parish that I miss the most. The acceptance by young people in the parish was particularly special to me. I am sure the experience of seeing the laity and clergy working together in such a collaborative manner had an effect on their understanding of what it means to be part of the church. And who knows? Maybe one of them is on her or his way to emerging as a future parish life coordinator.

◇◇◇

Notes

1. "Frequently Requested Catholic Church Statistics." Center for Applied Research in the Apostolate (CARA) at Georgetown University, http://www.cara.georgetown.edu/bulletin/index.htm (accessed on July 14, 2008).

2. Ibid.

3. Mark M. Gray and Mary L. Gautier, *Understanding the Trends II: Parish Life Coordinators in the United States.* Center for Applied Research in the Apostolate (CARA) at Georgetown University, p. 8.

4. Ibid, p. 6.

5. There are many different titles used for persons in these positions in dioceses. To simplify the presentation we selected one of the most commonly used.

6. "Frequently Requested Catholic Church Statistics," Ibid.

7. Carole Ganim, ed. *Shaping Catholic Parishes: Pastoral Leaders in the 21st Century,* p. 118–119.

8. "Frequently Requested Catholic Church Statistics," Ibid.

9. Mark Gray. From a talk given at the Emerging Models Project Symposium on Parish Life Coordinators, Sacramental Ministers, and Priest Moderators. Menlo Park, CA, January 8, 2007.

10. James A. Coriden, JCD, JD, "Parish Pastoral Leaders: Canonical Structures and Practical Questions," http://www.emergingmodels .org/doc/Articles/Corriden percent20on percent20PLCs.pdf (accessed July 14, 2008).

11. The Diocese of Colorado Springs uses the title "Parish Director."

12. Coriden, ibid.

13. Unless otherwise indicated, the data in this book is taken from the following sources: *Understanding the Ministry: Parish Life Coordinators in the United States*, (Washington: Emerging Models Project, 2005); Mark M. Gray and Mary L. Gautier, *Understanding the Trends II: Parish Life Coordinators in the United States*. Center for Applied Research in the Apostolate (CARA) at Georgetown University; and *Listening to the Spirit: Bishops and Parish Life Coordinators*, (Washington: Emerging Models Project, 2007).

14. My official title was "Parish Director."

15. Coriden, Ibid.

16. Coriden, p. 7.

17. Coriden, Ibid.

18. *Serving Shoulder to Shoulder*, Archdiocese of Los Angeles, (Los Angeles: 2006), p. 9.

19. *Listening to the Spirit: Bishops and Parish Life Coordinators*, (Washington: Emerging Models Project, 2007).,p.3.

20. *Shaping Catholic Parishes*, p. 70.

21. The designations in the CARA Project Report are configured from the regions established by the USCCB.

22. Peter Gilmour, *The Emerging Pastor*, (Kansas City: Sheed and Ward, 1986), p. 1.

23. The Archdiocese of Los Angeles uses the term "Parish Life Director" for this position.

24. *Serving Shoulder to Shoulder*, p. 9.

25. *As One Who Serves: A Pastoral Statement on Parish Leadership*, Archdiocese of Los Angeles. (Los Angeles: 2005), p. 1.

26. United States Catholic Conference of Bishops. Statistic quoted on Web site, www.usccb.org/laity.

27. *Catechism of the Catholic Church*, (Washington: 1997), no. 2179.

28. *As One Who Serves*, p. 8.

29. Ibid.

30. Kevin Treston, *Creative Christian Leadership: Skills for More Effective Ministry*, (Mystic: 1995), p. 18.

31. *Shaping Catholic Parishes*, p. 94.

32. Her title is Parish Life Director.

33. Henri Nouwen with Michael J. Christensen and Rebecca J. Laird, *Spiritual Direction: Wisdom for the Long Walk of Faith*, (New York: HarperCollins, 2006), p. 132.

34. Hans Finzel, *The Top Ten Mistakes That Leaders Make*, (Colorado Springs: 1994), p. 97.

35. Deborah Tannen, *You're Wearing That? Understanding Mothers and Daughters in Conversation*, (New York: Random House, 1995), p.13.

36. *Shaping Catholic Parishes*, p. 5.

37. From the compilation of feedback gathered at the Emerging Models Project Symposium on Parish Life Coordinators, February 2007.

38. Ibid., p. 110.

39. Loughlan Sofield, ST, and Carroll Juliano, SHCJ, *Collaboration: Uniting Our Gifts in Ministry*, (Notre Dame: Ave Maria Press, 2000), p. 17.

40. Kathy Hendricks, *Everything About Parish Ministry I Wish I Had Known*, (Denver: KMHendricks, Inc., 2007), p. 70.

41. Ibid., p. 115.

42. *Shaping Catholic Parishes*, p. 44.

43. Ibid., p. 76.

44. *Spiritual Direction*, p. 143.

45. Max Depree. *Leadership Jazz*, (New York: Dell, 1992), p. 171.

46. *Shaping Catholic Parishes*, p. 110–111.

47. Loughlan Soffield, Rosine Hammett, and Carroll Juliano, *Building Community* (Notre Dame: Ave Maria Press, 1998), p. 52.

48. "Parish Pastoral Leaders: Canonical Structures and Practical Questions," p. 15.

49. *Shaping Catholic Parishes*, pp. 103–104.

50. United States Conference of Catholic Bishops, *Co-Workers in the Vineyard of the Lord*, (Washington: 2005), p. 12.

51. *One Who Serves*, p. 4.

52. "Parish Pastoral Leaders: Canonical Structures and Practical Questions," p. 16.

53. Ibid., p. 15.

54. *Shaping Catholic Parishes*, pp. 120–121.

55. *As One Who Serves*, pp. 3–4.

56. *Building Community* (Notre Dame: 1998), p. 67.

57. Unites States Conference of Catholic Bishops, *United States Catholic Catechism for Adults*, p. 134.

Bibliography

Archdiocese of Los Angeles. *As One Who Serves: A Pastoral Statement on Parish Leadership*. Los Angeles: Archdiocese of Los Angeles, 2005.

———. *Serving Shoulder to Shoulder: Parish Life Directors in the Archdiocese of Los Angeles*. Los Angeles: Archdiocese of Los Angeles, 2006.

Bendyna, Mary, Mary Gautier, and Tricia Bruce. *Listening to the Spirit: Bishops and Parish Life Coordinators*. Washington: National Association for Lay Ministry, 2007.

Catechism of the Catholic Church. Washington: United States Catholic Conference, 1997.

Coriden, James A. "Parish Pastoral Leaders: Canonical Structures and Practical Questions." Emerging Models of Pastoral Leadership Project, http://www.emergingmodels.org (accessed July 14, 2008).

DePree, Max. *Leadership Jazz*. New York: Dell, 1992.

Finzel, Hans. *The Top Ten Mistakes That Leaders Make*. Colorado Springs: Cook Communications, 1994.

Ganim, Carole, ed. *Shaping Catholic Parishes: Pastoral Leaders in the 21st Century*. Chicago: Loyola Press, 2008.

Gilmour, Peter. *The Emerging Pastor*. Kansas City: Sheed and Ward, 1986.

Gray, Mark and Mary Gautier. *Understanding the Experience: A Profile of Lay Ecclesial Ministers Serving as Parish Life Coordinators*. Washington: National Association for Lay Ministry, 2004.

_____. *Understanding the Ministry: Parish Life Coordinators in the United States*. Washington: National Association for Lay Ministry, 2005.

_____. *Understanding the Trends: Parishes Entrusted to Parish Life Coordinators*. Washington: National Association for Lay Ministry, 2004.

Hendricks, Kathy. *Everything About Parish Ministry I Wish I Had Known*. Denver: KMHendricks, Inc., 2007.

Keating, Charles J. *The Leadership Book*. New York: Paulist Press, 1987.

Nouwen, Henri with Michael J. Christensen and Rebecca J. Laird. *Spiritual Direction: Wisdom for the Long Walk of Faith*. New York: HarperCollins, 2006.

Soffield, Loughlan and Carroll Juliano. *Collaboration: Uniting Our Gifts in Ministry*. Notre Dame: Ave Maria Press, 2000.

_____. *Collaborative Ministry: Skills and Guidelines*. Notre Dame: Ave Maria Press, 1987.

Soffield, Loughlan, Rosine Hammett, and Carroll Juliano, *Building Community*. Notre Dame: Ave Maria Press, 1998.

Swain, Bernard. *Liberating Leadership: Practical Styles for Pastoral Ministry*. New York: Harper & Row, 1986.

Tannen, Deborah. *Talking From 9 to 5*. New York: Avon, 1995.

_____. *You're Wearing That? Understanding Mothers and Daughters in Conversation*. New York: Random House, 2006.

Treston, Kevin. *Creative Christian Leadership: Skills for More Effective Ministry*. Mystic: Twenty-Third Publications, 1995.

United States Conference of Catholic Bishops. *Co-Workers in the Vineyard of the Lord*. 2005.

United States Conference of Catholic Bishops. *United States Catholic Catechism for Adults*. 2006.

The Project: Emerging Models of Pastoral Leadership

The Emerging Models of Pastoral Leadership Project studied the use of Canon 517.2. A series of studies was conducted for the Project by the Center of Applied Research in the Apostolate (CARA), under the direction of lead researcher Mark Gray, Ph.D. A series of focus groups of bishops were also conducted for the Project by CARA, based on a protocol developed by a committee of canonists and theologians. In addition, two invitational symposiums were hosted under the direction of a committee made up of members of the National Association for Lay Ministry, the National Association of Diaconate Directors, and the National Federation of Priests' Councils. Although this model of pastoral leadership has been in use since the early 1980s only a small amount of research had taken place. Today there is a growing understanding of this ministry along with an increased awareness of the ecclesiological issues around the use of this canon. The top recommendations of the National Ministry Summit, hosted by the Emerging Models Project, included the request for the bishops to define the titles, roles, and responsibilities of those engaged in this ministry.

From 2003 through 2008, the Emerging Models of Pastoral Leadership Project, a collaborative effort of six national organizations, funded by the Lilly Endowment, Inc., conducted national research on the emerging models of parish and parish leadership, including the emerging phenomenon known as "parish life coordinators." The six partner organizations of the Emerging Models of Pastoral Leadership Project include the:

- National Association for Lay Ministry
- Conference for Pastoral Planning and Council Development
- National Association of Church Personnel Administrators
- National Association of Diaconate Directors
- National Catholic Young Adult Ministry Association
- National Federation of Priests' Councils

Together, these six ministerial organizations conducted a series of research initiatives including studies of lay ecclesial ministry, Canon 517.2 leadership, multiple parish pastoring, human resource issues, the next generation of pastoral leaders; and best practices for parishes and parish leaders. Information on each of these initiatives is available on the Emerging Models Project Website: http://www.emergingmodels.org.

Marti R. Jewell
Project Director

About the Author

Kathy Hendricks has more than twenty-five years of experience in catechetical and pastoral ministry, having served in parishes and dioceses in Colorado, Alaska, and British Columbia. She served as parish life coordinator of Pax Christi Parish in Littleton, Colorado, and was the Director of Religious Education for the Diocese of Colorado Springs for six years. Her books include *Everything About Parish Ministry I Wish I Had Known* and *A Parent's Guide to Prayer.*